PROBLEM SOLVING
in the
Christian
Family

PROBLEM SOLVING in the Christian Family

by David A. Seamands

Creation House
Carol Stream, Illinois

First printing—August, 1975
Second printing—August, 1976

ISBN 0-88419-109-5
Library of Congress Catalog Card Number 75-3610

To my wife

Helen

Whose love helped to create
our three greatest problems
and then to turn them into
our three greatest joys:

Sharon
Steve
Debbie

CONTENTS

Introduction:

The American Family Tragedy

"Honey, Ted and Harriet are getting a divorce."
"You've got to be kidding! We just finished celebrating their 17th anniversary with them. I mean, of all our friends, they seemed to have the most going for them..."

Sound familiar? It *is* all too familiar. Never before have so many men and women been putting asunder what God hath joined together. One out of every three marriages this year will terminate in the divorce courts. And the rate is increasing. In some areas of the country, it is already higher than that. Today in Los Angeles, of every twelve marriages, ten end in divorce.

As tragic as the high rate of divorce is, in reality the great state of marriage is in even worse shape. Sociologists concede that *two* out of three marriages would end in divorce were it not for the children. And if the high cost and difficult procedures in most states were removed, along with what's left of the rapidly-diminishing social stigma, their projection might be even higher.

Unhappily, the statistics are borne out by personal experience. Think of the homes you know that are living graveyards of former love and hope, where all communication on the heart level between husband and

9

wife ceased years ago, where they escape from one another into the newspaper or television or the phone or busyness, and the essence of their conversation at dinner is, "Pass the potatoes," or an angry outburst at the kids. It could be that the people in Los Angeles are more honest than many in the rest of the country.

From the Christian point of view—and that is from where I am writing this book—the saddest thing of all is that Christian marriages are not immune. Husbands and wives who know that Jesus was—and is—the Son of God, and who have been told countless times, and perhaps have even told others that He is the answer to any problem, are finding themselves locked into bitterness, apathy, and even hatred. More and more are deciding that despite the fact that it goes directly against the Word of God, divorce is the only way out.

Why is the American family breaking down? A recent survey by *Better Homes and Gardens* is worth looking at, not because the magazine is particularly noted for its sociological perception, but because the unusually large response to a questionnaire sent to their readers—340,370 replies—insures a representative opinion. One finding stands out: *the vast percentage agree that religion is losing its influence on American life.*

In two generations, a nation that was founded *by men who* so *trusted* in God that they said so on their money, now has little time for Him. There are no statistics here of course, but it wouldn't surprise me if nine out of ten men who first came to this country put God's will before all else. Today, it would be encouraging to find one in ten who do.

Unfortunately, there is no such thing as a spiritual vacuum. Where God is no longer central, the world, the flesh and the devil are quick to take up position. Rebellion has become a fashionable thing—a healthy expression of one's individuality, almost a national ideal.

Meanwhile, submission is decidedly unfashionable, a sign of weakness. This is true even in many Christian circles. We ignore the fact that it was Lucifer's rebellion which got him tossed out of heaven. Rebellion versus submission to God's will and order has been man's supreme struggle ever since.

"Nevertheless, not my will but Thy will be done . . ." Christian man has been battling for centuries to put down his own will for God's. Yet now, in the face of a relentless barrage of propaganda promoting the glamor, the integrity and even the duty of rebellion on all sides, the good fight seems less worth expending all one's might for than ever before.

The result is a New Morality that many young people today might sum up: "If it feels good, do it." Those with still-twitching consciences might insert "and if it doesn't hurt anyone." What or whoever impinges upon your freedom, or hampers the free expression of your personality—be it the boss or teachers or parents or civil authorities or God or whoever is in charge—is to be rebelled against; openly if possible, covertly in any event.

What effect has the New Morality had on the 1970's attitude towards marriage? We don't hear so much about marriage itself these days; we hear of open marriage and trial marriage and premarital marriage and "viable alternatives to marriage."

Other factors have contributed to the plight of the American family.

Mobility is one: we have become a nation of corporate gypsies. According to the latest findings of the Family Service Association of America, the average American family moves *fourteen* times in a lifetime, or once every four or five years. Many men working for large corporations find themselves moving more frequently.

Gone are the roots and friendships, the family ties and traditions that were such a part of the fabric of our lives. Gone, too, is much of the sense of permanence and worth and belonging that went with them.

Another is the departure of mothers from the home. More than twenty per cent of all American women with

11

children of preschool age are working outside their homes today. This is not to say it is wrong for mothers to work. Studies show that the decisive factor is not whether a mother works; both decency and delinquency can come out of either type home. But a mother's absence can remove one more pinion of a family's stability.

What, then, are the three great enemies of the American family today—or of any family anywhere, for that matter?

Idolatry is the most obvious, and by idolatry I mean a false sense of values.

Call it secularism or materialism, it is the belief that the important thing is what a family's home *has,* instead of what that home *is.* It is often said that this is a product of our affluent society. But don't let that mislead you. I have seen some of the poorest people in the world as enslaved by this sort of idolatry as the well-to-do. In fact, their very poverty can tend to make them intensely materialistic, and some of the most thing-worshiping people I know are those whose parents came from extremely poor homes. Now that they are grown and well off, they bend over backwards to make certain their children have every conceivable material advantage.

How often I have heard this from those in trouble.

"Oh, yes, my parents gave me everything! I had all the toys and allowance I wanted, my own beautiful room, and later a car and—they even gave me a lot of things I didn't ask for. They gave me everything—everything, that is, except love and understanding and guidelines for choosing values in life."

The Christian home is not invulnerable to this strange paradox of false values. We Christians are so careful to have the best and most beautiful of things and are so careless about the spiritual quality of our homes. We make sacrifices for air-conditioning and cannot sacrifice fifteen minutes' sleep for prayer-conditioning.

What I am talking about is a spiritual astigmatism where values are upside down.

12

This can hurt our homes from the sacred and religious side as well. How many parents have we seen who have been so busy working for God and the church that their own children have been neglected? We can work to save the world and lose those nearest us.

The Bible warns against this. In the Epistles, when a man was examined to ascertain whether he was fit to be a pastor or presiding elder, one of the first things to come under scrutiny was his family life. How were things in his home?

It is a problem my wife and I faced during our sixteen years as missionaries. Talk about working mothers, how in the world do you maintain a Christian home when both parents are able to see their children only three months out of the year? It just isn't possible, except in Christ—all things are possible.

My parents were also missionaries, and they faced the same problem, having to be away from us for years at a time. Yet if you are in God's perfect will, the grace will be there. I can truly say that I came from a Christ-centered home. He was there, and I knew my parents were there, too, in spirit if not in the flesh.

The answer lies in the quality of Christian relationship maintained in the home. The Christian home is not a matter of quantity, but quality.

The Christian home is a place where Christ's order of values is paramount, with the primacy of the personal in the giving of time or a listening, loving ear to our children's problems when we are with them. And if ensuring that the right spirit is present in the home, no matter how much we have to be away, means an occasional disruption of schedule or a rearranging of priorities, then so be it. More than once I have dropped everything to go home and get things straightened out.

This business of the right spirit in the home cannot be overstressed. Family devotions, personal prayer times, meaningful grace before meals—such observances are helpful. But when your children are grown, and everyone

13

seems to be living on a different schedule, coordination is often not possible. The best forms of worship, if devoid of the right spirit, are void indeed.

The key is maintaining a home in which the atmosphere is one of everyone living in the presence of God's love—a home in which *all* activities are considered sacred. Obviously such an atmosphere must originate with husband and wife, and it takes effort and determination and deep personal commitment. But the results—a sense of true values and a grounding in the Lordship of Jesus—are worth it all.

The second great enemy of the home, which is spreading like an insidious virus across the land, is *infidelity.*

Here I am using the term in its comprehensive sense, including thought and word, as well as deed. As such, it encompasses all the places where the New Morality has deadened our Christian sensitivity and ridiculed the Biblical basis of our beliefs.

TV has become full of off-color humor and the acceptance of promiscuous behavior as the norm. But what is most indicative are the subtle ways in which the basic standards of marital fidelity are ridiculed or openly mocked. And what makes it serious is that between the ages of three and eighteen, the average American spends 22,000 hours a year watching TV. (That same average young American, if he happens to be a better-than-average churchgoer, will spend only 3,000 hours in Sunday School and other church-related activities.)

Today's television glamorizes infidelity. In emotion-manipulating melodrama, in cleverly wrapped puns, on talk shows, proud of their candor, the idea of promiscuous sex is promoted.

Into our homes, then, has come something which is undercutting the very foundation of Christian marriage which is *the commitment to mutual, exclusive love.* Jesus made this the basic requirement for a Christian family, yet the spirit of infidelity has slithered so far into our minds

14

that, though a man may never act upon the wandering of his imagination, it has never been so difficult for him to refuse every wayward thought. It can be done. The fusillade of suggestive stimuli can be withstood. But it takes more grace and grit and grounding than ever before in Christendom.

The grace is up to God, but the grit and grounding are our department, and we have got to deliver in the middle of a moral wasteland so chaotic it literally defies description. Vance Packard entitled his recent book *The Sexual Wilderness,* rather than use the operative phrase, "The Sexual Revolution," because he confides in his foreword, revolution implies a movement with a specific goal. It is in the midst of this trackless wilderness that our Christian homes must become oases of life and love, instilling in our children Biblical standards of moral purity and marital fidelity.

The third great enemy of the American home is *indiscipline.*

Here again we are tasting the fruit of the wholesale abandonment of Scriptural principles in the past two generations; in this case, in favor of the tenets of modern child psychology. "Discipline inhibits a child . . . given complete freedom, a child will order his own life, and he should have every opportunity to express himself (which is a little like letting a garden express itself—and winding up with a stunning crop of weeds!) . . . rather than ever forcing a child to do our will instead of his own, we should reason with him, as if he were an equal . . ."

What a lot of nonsense! But the "enlightened" parents of the mid-twentieth century swallowed it all as part of the wonderful legacy of the New Scientific Age. Those were heady days! The first jet airplanes, nuclear energy, penicillin, DDT, psychoanalysis—man was on the verge of mastering his environment. Technology became our god.

Nor did its high priests, the scientists and engineers and utopians, discourage such adulation.

15

"Give us enough time and money and goodwill, and we will solve all your problems," they said.

And for a while, it looked as though they might. But somehow, there never seemed to be enough time and money, and goodwill was little more than a sentiment on Christmas cards. Moreover, each solution they did come up with created ten more problems that no one had been able to foresee. When called to account, these same men absolved themselves of the very responsibility they once were so ready to assume by saying, "Well, we're not God, are we?"

Clearly not. Yet it wasn't long before more than a few equated them as such and raised their children accordingly. Then they stood by and watched these same children, now so rooted in their rebellion, tear apart campus after campus across the country. They convulsively lashed out at the nearest representatives of authority, or indulged in an emotional orgy of mindless activism. They turned the violence—the inherent result of rebellion's inexorably embittering disillusionment—inward upon themselves in the form of escape drugs and dropped out of society by countless thousands. They proved to have adult bodies, but the emotional maturity of pre-adolescents.

Now, even Dr. Spock has admitted that he might have been wrong. Only it's a little late. Across America, millions of kids have already left home, in spirit, if not in fact. Parents have abdicated their position as authorities, trusting that the schools and churches would somehow fill the gap. However, since the exercising of authority is not the primary function of schools and churches, they have not filled the gap. Therefore, as noted before, rebellion is still in fashion.

Discipline—the word has its roots in the meaning of "disciple." A disciple is one who follows a way, and anyone serious about following Jesus has to begin by denying himself. "If anyone wishes to come after Me, let him deny himself, and take up his cross daily (denying oneself is seldom painless), and follow Me" (Luke 9:23). No child is ever going to deny himself voluntarily without a good deal of training.

The key concept can be found in these words: "And you shall teach them diligently to your sons" (Deuteronomy 6:7) and "Train up a child in the way he should go" (Proverbs 22:6).

"Teach" and "train"—a parent should see himself not as a judge or commanding officer or policeman, and not in a buddy-buddy role, either. He should see himself as a teacher. It is in the role of teacher and trainer that parenthood takes its ordained place in God's scheme of things.

As a teacher, it is your responsibility to fill the two greatest needs of your child's life: *great love* and *definite limits*. Dozens of books have been written about the former; very little has been said about the latter, at least in this century. But if you fail to teach your child limits, you fail to train him to deal with reality for this is a world of cause and effect, of choices and consequences. Every good instructor will teach the limits that this order of things imposes on us and will care enough for the child to reinforce the learning process with punishment, if necessary.

Love and limits, affection and discipline, must go side by side.

True parental love cares so deeply for the child that it will not tolerate wrong ways of behavior, ways that someday could well destroy the child. There is no greater or more revealing test of our Christian lives and parenthood than how we handle this whole matter of discipline. Suffice it to say that if a child is disciplined in the right spirit, he will know that the parent loves him, even as know that "Whom the Lord loves, He disciplines" (Hebrews 12:6).

Idolatry, infidelity, and *indiscipline* are the three great enemies of the American home. Taken together, they seem almost overpowering, making it beyond our capacity to avert the American family tragedy.

But God had a plan. And He still does.

I trust that in the following pages I can show you how I have seen this plan work out.

David A. Seamands
Wilmore, Kentucky

1

"In the Beginning . . ."

In times of great stress, when all human resources prove pathetically inadequate, man in desperation turns back to his Maker, and implores His aid or comfort. Some do so in profound repentance for ever having turned away. Most who turn His way do so because there is no other way *to* turn.

Usually this turning (or returning) comes in the wake of some natural disaster, epidemic, war or other man-made catastrophe. Today the American family stands directly in the path of a tidal wave of moral corruption. Its forerunners have already hit and inundated us and left us gasping. But if Biblical prophecy is correct (and it hasn't been wrong yet), they are nothing compared to the mountainous wave which is already high on the horizon and is bearing down on us.

Among those with eyes to see it coming, the basic reactions are apathy and alarm. The former may already be in the majority. There is a growing attitude that if moral rape is inevitable, then relax and enjoy it. But for those who are still concerned, two courses of action are open: man's way and God's way.

Man's way says, "Don't just stand there (or kneel there), do something! Boycott! March! Pass legislation!"

Only it's hard to legislate against what the legislators have just finished legislating in favor of. Prohibition proved the impossibility of trying to force other men to behave in a way they were hell-bent on not behaving in. Repeal acknowledged that. Today man is no different. As we witnessed in 1974, the thinking of the New Morality permeated the highest echelons of civil authority.

Where can we *escape*?

Is there a town or an island that is both practical and beyond the reach of today's mental, physical and spiritual pollution? Can we, in fact, get away at all? Or is the cancer already so embedded that we take it with us?

The Robinson Crusoe syndrome has tremendous romantic appeal, but a fresh look at the classic reveals two things: the rigors of roughing it in the wild are harrowing indeed for the fittest and most resourceful of men. But to brave them alone, without God, is to risk insanity or an early demise or both. (Crusoe was a devout Christian, who sought God's will before any undertaking.)

Which brings us back to our second course of action: *when all else fails, read the instructions.*

Someone once referred to the Bible as the Manufacturer's Handbook. Let's see what it has to say about the family, how it was first put together, what its function is, and what it takes to keep it running smoothly. For while God may well call His children into unified action of one sort or another, the first—and last—bastion against the onslaught of the New Morality is the integrity of the Christian home.

When reading the instructions it is best to start at the beginning, particularly since Jesus Himself, every time He was asked questions about marriage and the family, went back to the Genesis account in the Bible.

"In the beginning God created the heavens and the earth," reads the first verse in the Bible (Genesis 1:1). This is a good reminder that, regardless of the speculations of sociologists and anthropologists, the family began in the mind of God.

Actually, Christians have no quarrel with the scientific explanation for the basis of the family (as far as it goes). It is a biological fact that human beings feel the urge to reproduce at all times and not just in certain seasons, and young human offspring have the longest period of helplessness—of total dependence on their parents—of any species.

But these two cause-and-effect observations cannot begin to tap the significance of the family, because they ignore the Prime Cause. The family derives its importance, its ultimate value, from the fact that it originated in God. It did not just happen. God designed and created it, and nothing is clearer than this in the Genesis record.

If we take the first and second chapters of Genesis together, this is the picture of the family that emerges: The first chapter (Genesis 1:27) says, "And God created man in His own image." Men have a habit of stopping there, without finishing the verse: "*male and female* He created them." And then He charged his new creations to bear children and multiply, and He gave them dominion over all the plants and animals of the earth.

And so, we have the first of the three purposes of the family: *procreation.*

If we break that word into two thoughts, "pro" and "create," we see that it means to create on behalf of. God alone is the Creator, but in verse 28, He is inviting man and woman to share with Him the wonder, mystery and glory of creation, and has entrusted into their hands the power to continue the work of His creation.

The details of God's creation of the family are supplied in the second chapter of Genesis. Having created man and given him dominion over every lesser being, "Then the Lord God said, 'It is not good for the man to be alone, I will make a helper suitable for him' " (Genesis 2:18).

How perfectly God understands man's need for *companionship*, the second purpose of the family.

True to His word, God performed what some have

referred to as "the first surgical operation under anesthesia," taking a part of man and making for him a partner. Interestingly, Dr. Crawford Long, one of the co-discoverers of modern anesthesia, said that the idea for putting a patient to sleep under ether first came to him while he was sitting in church, listening to a sermon on the text, "So the Lord God caused a deep sleep to fall upon the man" (Genesis 2:21).

Then in what appears to be the first marriage ceremony, with God Himself acting as the officiating minister, we read in Genesis 2:22, "The Lord God brought her unto the man." Thus united with woman, man felt his completeness and his wholeness, and with a burst of joyous inspiration, he provided the Bible with its first poetry: "And the man said, 'This is now bone of my bones, And flesh of my flesh; She shall be called *woman,* Because she was taken out of Man' " (Genesis 2:23).

Now man had someone to share with, to touch and love and help and be helped by. Now he had companionship. And in the next verse, the Word of God explains that "for this cause a man shall leave his father and his mother, and shall cleave to his wife; (as the woman is henceforth referred to), and they shall become one flesh" (Genesis 2:24).

The third purpose of the family is to provide *nurture.*

As God joins two people together in holy wedlock for the purpose of companionship and entrusts them with the power to procreate, He also blesses their union with children. And with them, He confers the awesome responsibility for protecting them and providing for them, for teaching them and training them up to become mature members of God's family in their own right, ready and equipped to one day undertake the same responsibility themselves.

The ideal Christian family is one which fulfills these purposes in accordance with God's guidelines, and is a place of mutual love and affection for every member of the family. The reason it is given such great emphasis throughout the Bible is because it is absolutely central to God's plan. There is a saying that something is true just because it's in the Bible. More accurately it is in the Bible because it *is* true.

Here is one point on which modern psychologists are also in rare agreement: the enormous, even frightening importance of the home in shaping the human personality. The first few years of a child's life, they say, are the most crucial in determining habits of behavior, as well as the set of character.

But before we can talk about God's plan for the raising of children, before we can consider what makes—or breaks—a Christian marriage, we need to go back to where it all begins. In the beginning, two people are in love and desire to spend the rest of their lives together. Or one person is in love with love and is whirling around like a cocked proton, looking for a likely neutron to latch onto and form a nucleus.

2

So You Want To
Get Married

"Dearly Beloved, we are gathered together here in the sight of God . . . ," the minister intones.

The bride is a shimmering vision of loveliness, the groom beside her, tall and erect, her father behind her, the wedding party on either side . . . . Everything dissolves into a hazy, gossamer dream—until the jubilant opening chords of Mendelssohn's wedding march peal forth, and everyone blinks away the last tear and breaks into a grin.

And so, that first marriage in Genesis, with all its awe and holiness and gratitude and joy, is repeated today. But today this most beautiful of all ceremonies and the union that it consecrates have become the magic solution in the eyes of so many frustrated, unhappy young people that there is a headlong rush to get married that bowls over all reason and insight in its path.

Adolescent infatuation, peer-group pressure, security, rebellion—the list of wrong reasons grows longer, and each one is responsible for untold misery and bitterness. You can warn them, yet they never seem to learn, and you can spot the anxious ones among the singles of any congregation: the ambitious young man with his life all planned out and needing only a wife to get on to the next plateau . . . the bride's wistful-eyed older sister, wondering if the promise of the bouquet she has just caught will ever be fulfilled . . .

A favorite story of mine is the one about the no-longer-so-young woman who, beginning to panic at the prospect of spending the rest of her life making dinner for one, went to see her pastor. Unfortunately, this worthy, like so many of our species, elected to hide behind some very pious platitudes. "My dear, you may rest assured that the Lord has a plan: one woman for every man, and one man for every woman. Now one can't very well improve on that, can one?"

"Improve on it?" his earnest visitor replied. "Pastor, I don't want to improve on it. I just want to get in on it!"

Not to hide behind any pious platitudes, comforting cliches, or sentimental shibboleths, let it be said right off that the American scheme of dating and courtship is often a ruthless and risky business, one that is loaded with injustices, particularly for the woman, who must somehow walk the narrow line between attractiveness and seduction, warm availability and coy disinterest. It is a system that leaves much to be desired, and statistically it hasn't had a very good record. But it's all we have, and so all we can do is make the best possible Christian decisions within the framework of our particular cultural context.

Unfortunately, here is one place where we can't go to the Bible for specific illustrations that might be of help, because in the days in which the Scriptures were written, marriages were largely a matter of parental arrangement. But we can always go there for definite Scriptural principles, and there are a number which pertain.

In this business of choosing the right mate, there are two major errors to avoid, the first of which I call the *Hollywood error*.

We have been sold a false bill of goods by our sensate climate, namely, that love is an overwhelming rush of feeling that sweeps over you with such intensity it simply *impels* you into the decision to marry. Rubbish! Some personalities may work that way. Most don't. *Some people have great feelings that sweep them into commitment. Others have to make great commitments and experience the sweep of feelings later.* Don't wait for the Hollywood surge of love. It might be love, but it could also be overactive glands.

The other pitfall to avoid is the *heavenly error,* which is waiting for God to make the decision for you. I have some startling news for you: if you *are* waiting for Him to make up your mind for you, you may die single. *God does not choose your mate for you!* He will guide you along the way, and if you are willing to listen, He can keep you from making a tragic mistake. But in the last analysis, the final decision is yours and yours alone.

So do not expect God to write in lightning in the sky, "Marry Mary."

And don't put out a fleece and expect the wool to be dyed with a special message saying, "Marry Harry."

You are not a puppet. God gave you free will, and this is one of those major turning-point decisions where you are going to have to exercise it and assume full responsibility for the ultimate decision, "for better, for worse," as the ceremony puts it.

Sure, it's harder. It takes faith! Proverbs 3:6 says, *"In all your ways acknowledge Him, and He will make your paths straight."* And it's *true,* but the only way you are going to find that out is by having the faith to step out. Someone else put it another way: there's a riverboat tied up at a dock. It has a rudder, but the only way that rudder is going to be able to guide that boat is if the boat pushes off from the dock and moves out into midstream.

As Christians, we know that God has promised to lead us by giving us special insight to make the right choices in life. To me this is one of the most wonderful things about being a Christian: the sense of being guided day by day, decision by decision. The Bible is full of concrete examples of divine guidance, and when you talk to Christians, almost all would agree: "Well, as I look back over my life, there can be no doubt that God had His hand on me."

The trouble is, what they're saying is that they believe in guidance in reverse, and what we're talking about here is something much more difficult: getting God's guidance *beforehand,* so that we can make a decision in accordance with His will and plan for us.

In making any major decision, there are two things to keep in mind. First, never make it on the strength of just one avenue of guidance, but base it on *cumulative evidence.* Second, have the patience to *wait upon God* and not act until you have peace in your heart that you have made as right a decision as could be made under the circumstances.

3

God's Measuring Stick

What do we mean by cumulative evidence? In her great classic, *The Christian's Secret of a Happy Life,* Hannah Whitehall Smith has an excellent chapter on guidance for making a decision. In it she says there are four voices which must be in agreement. Since the Speaker is always the same (God), if there is a contradiction, then you know that at least one of the voices is not of the Lord, because God does not contradict Himself. While affirming her four voices, I would also add a fifth.

The first voice is *the Scriptures,* and they are first because they are the written and spoken Word of God.

We are not talking about a single, isolated verse here. In searching the Scriptures, occasionally a single verse will seem to stand out, but we need to be very careful: it is Satan who quotes Scripture (in Luke 4) single verse by single verse. And it is Jesus who answers him with the balanced whole of God's Word.

God does tolerate Biblical "lucky dipping" in beginning Christians, but after a brief season or the moment such a device becomes a crutch or a shortcut, He removes all grace from it. Much of the fanaticism I have encountered has resulted when some isolated verse has been taken from context and emphasized out of all proportion, to support things that actually run counter to the spirit and general principles of the Bible. *Balance* is the watchword for mature Christians.

The second source of guidance should be an *inner voice*.

These interior impressions can indeed be the "still, small voice" of the Holy Spirit; they can also be from Satan, who is a master of deception. It takes a lot of careful listening—and walking through—for the sheep to begin to know the voice of his Shepherd. On major decisions, these inner voices should *always* be checked against the other sources of guidance, preferably the witness of a counselor or other mature Christian, because they can also emanate from a third source: a powerful self-will, which most of us have. We want what we want when we want it, and we are pretty fair masters at deceiving ourselves that God is telling us we're supposed to have it.

That's why it is so handy to be able to check out our guidance with another person. Only here, too, some caution is advisable, for strong personalities can also be too persuasive. Again, the watchword is balance. If we are sincere and in need, the Lord will direct our path to a counselor with proven wisdom and discernment.

The third voice is *providential circumstance*.

God often matches inner impressions with outward circumstances. Open-door/closed-door guidance may seem crude or simplistic, but it's very effective, and it's hard to misinterpret. Even so, it, too, should be weighed in the balance with the other avenues. The problem with fleeces, which are also in this category, is that we have a way of interpreting them just the way we want them to come out. This is especially true of courtship.

The fourth voice is *our reason*. I am not speaking here merely of our unaided human reason, for we all have had the experience of being absolutely certain we were right, only to find out later that we were wrong. I am talking about what E. Stanley Jones calls "our heightened moral

29

intelligence"—a calm, Spirit-controlled consideration of all the facts involved.

The fifth voice is the witness of *other people.*

This could be a counselor, a trusted friend, or a personal prayer group of which you are a member. It could even be a large group such as your church as a whole. The Book of Acts is filled with illustrations like, "For it seemed good to the Holy Spirit and to us" (Acts 15:28a). If these five voices are all weighed carefully, the cumulative evidence should be fairly clear.

But it isn't always, or right away, and that's when we must have the patient determination to "wait upon the Lord"—*until there is agreement of all five voices, or at least most of them, so that He confirms and strengthens us in our inner assurance that we have arrived at the right decision.* God's guidance is cumulative and progressive, often the forging of one link after another into a chain, until the whole is complete and convincing. In quietness and patience we must wait until we come to the place where we have real peace about it, and it is extremely unwise to move while our spirit is still troubled or agitated. I love Paul's verse on this: "And let the peace of Christ rule in your hearts" (Colossians 3:15).

Now, to be of some assistance to the fourth voice, the voice of reason, it has been my marital and pre-marital counseling experience that there are three main areas to consider in this business of choosing a mate.

Spiritual oneness is the first.

Here God comes into the picture in a very real and definite way. "Do not be bound together with unbelievers" (II Corinthians 6:14). This means that if you truly put Christ first in your life, you are not free to choose a non-Christian mate.

"Do two men walk together unless they have an appointment?" asks Amos (3:3) and follows it with a firm negative answer. Then how in the world could they live together in the most intimate of all human relationships? "They cannot," God says, and while He will not choose your mate for you, He *will* help by making it clear whom you should *not* marry; in this case, an unbeliever. Your mate must be someone who is one with you spiritually.

The second area to consider is *vocational concurrence.* Here again, God comes into the picture in a very definite way. What do you feel is God's call on your life, His specific will for you?

Can the circle of God's will for you and His will for your prospective mate overlap? Or are you called to be a missionary to Zaire but she feels called to be a teacher in Taiwan? If so, you may make a lovely couple, very fond of one another, but it is obvious you are not for each other.

From my experience on the mission field, I can assure you that vocational agreement *is* important. Many a life has been wrecked because a young person was not careful enough at this point. In all fairness, however, I must add that very few young women have such a specific call in their lives. Most of them have only a general call and a willingness to do God's will. They receive the specifics of their call through their husband, usually in support of his ministry.

4

You Must Choose

We have seen that God does not choose for us, but now we are seeing that He does prescribe the *type* of person whom we cannot marry. It is like giving you a wide circle of freedom and saying that you may make your choice among any within that circle.

Does that have a familiar ring to it? "*But* from the fruit of the tree which is in the middle of the garden . . ." (Genesis 3:3a). Years ago, I was sympathetic when someone would come to me for counsel about being in love and wanting to marry an unbeliever. I am no longer. I have seen too much tragedy as a result.

I dislike hurting feelings, but I have found that it is far kinder in the long run to be blunt at the outset. If a Christian who wants to marry an unbeliever tells me he is praying about it and asking God to show them definitely, I tell him to stop wasting his time. God has already told him. And God is not about to deny His Word, so don't bother asking Him to.

Let me share a letter with you.

". . . In my second year at college, I came to you once for counseling. You may not even remember me. I was going with a young man who was not a Christian and wanted your advice. You told me that perhaps I could go on with him and maybe he would change, but that was living in unreality.

"You also told me that, if I were patient and true to my faith, I would surely find someone who would be God's will for me. Well, with many tears I broke up with that fellow, but by the peace I had in my heart, I knew I was doing God's perfect will.

"Doc, I want to thank you so much for that advice which kept me from making the biggest mistake of my life. Now I praise God for His working in my life, and I want you to know that God has led me, and I have found the most wonderful life partner."

The letter goes on to tell an interesting and unusual story of how this girl and her husband met, and of their happiness in a Christian marriage.

Let us now suppose that you have found someone who likes the idea of spending the rest of his life with you as much as you do with him, and with whom you are in spiritual and vocational agreement. There is still one more area to consider before you make the final decision.

That is *personality blending*—your basic social, intellectual, emotional and family compatibility.

Here are the practical, down-to-earth realities that make up the personality blend which can result in a livable Christian family relationship:

Do we have the same general economic and social outlook on life?

Does he or she have the qualities that I want to see in my children?

Do I have real respect for him or her?

Is this the kind of person I want to look at across the breakfast table for the next forty years?

Just how well do we get along under pressure?

Can we communicate well?

Can I really share myself with him or her?

Do I accept him or her as he or she is?

Does he accept me as I am?

Or do either of us have a desire to change the other in order to make him easier to love?

Dr. Clifford Adams, the former director of the Marriage Counseling Service at Pennsylvania State College, suggests this set of questions as a quick indicator of whether a person is truly in love or just infatuated by good looks and sex appeal:

1. Do you have a great number of things you like to do together?
2. Do you have a feeling of pride when you compare your friend with anyone else you know?
3. Do you suffer from a feeling of unrest when away from him/her?
4. Even when you quarrel, do you still enjoy being together?
5. Have you a strong desire to please him/her, and are you quite glad to give way on your own preferences?
6. Do you actually want to marry this person?
7. Does he/she have the qualities you would like to have in your children?
8. Do your friends and associates admire this person and think he would be a good match for you?
9. Do your parents think you are in love? (They're very discerning about such things.)
10. Have you started planning, at least in your own mind, what kind of wedding, children, and home you will have?

If you can truthfully answer *yes* to at least seven of the above, then Dr. Adams's diagnosis would be that you are in love.

So now, let us assume that, having weighed carefully all the aforementioned considerations, you are engaged to be married. *Now* is the time for the two of you to take a long, hard look at what marriage is all about, and at what it is going to take to make your marriage work. If you already are married and your marriage is in trouble or not all that it should be, now is a good time to go back to the basics.

5

The Heart of a Christian Marriage

"Whether you marry or not, you will regret it."—*Socrates*

But then, Socrates did not have Jesus, and wisdom drawn from the deepest well, if that well is not fed by the springs of Living Water, cannot help but turn sour in the cup.

The greatest thing that any Christian marriage has going for it is Jesus Christ. With Him, no obstacle is insurmountable, no marriage is too far gone. That is the single, most important truth in this book.

Jesus can be invited into the home of a dead marriage, take that marriage by the hand, and restore it to life. What's more, He can rebuild it, stone by stone, into undreamed-of wholeness, on a rock foundation of openness, honesty and trust. And that is not just a hope; it is the testimony of countless thousands of marriages, which, in their death-throes, had invited Him in when He knocked at the door.

Jesus can shatter the bondage of reciprocal vindictiveness and replace it with His love. He can banish the mists of fantasy in favor of daylight reality with Him. He can be our all-sufficiency, no matter how deep the yearning, and He can close ancient, bleeding wounds without leaving a scar. *He is able.*

And how greatly He cares! For those who know Him, He is there from the beginning, chief among the wedding guests, blessing and sealing the sacred instructions, as His surrogate solemnly joins them together in holy matrimony—

"Which is an honorable estate, instituted of God, and signifying to us the mystical union that exists between Christ and His Church; which holy estate Christ adorned and beautified with His presence in Cana of Galilee . . ."

You can almost sense His presence in the words. Though I have officiated at many weddings, the solemnity of the occasion never fails to impress me. When I grip the hands of bride and groom and say, "I now pronounce you husband and wife," a strange and awesome feeling goes through me, as if His hands had joined with ours. I know that others at weddings feel the same way—conscious that they are standing on holy ground.

We don't feel that way about other human transactions. Why such reverence and wonder at weddings? Partly because marriage is so important in God's eyes, and partly because of the enormity of the consequences involved.

Think about it: two people who have never lived together before say a few words to each other, sign a piece of paper, and then undertake to live together for the rest of their lives. They have begun something completely new and wonderful and their union most often will result in the birth of human beings who would never have been born if they had not made that particular decision.

From now on, the suffering of one will become the suffering of the other; the joy of one will become happiness for the other. If the husband fails in his chosen profession, the humiliation and economic burden will fall upon his wife as well. If one of them falls into disgrace, the other will share the embarrassment. The risk involved is tremendous, for each partner is now vulnerable to the other's sorrows as well as his joys, and the potential for both is equally great.

The stakes could not be higher, and the game is for keeps. *"It is, therefore, not to be entered into unadvisedly, but reverently, discreetly, and in the fear of God."*

This being the case, it is astonishing to me how many young people hang onto the myth that they don't need to know anything about marriage or what is going to be required of them, that somehow their great love is enough to see them through. It is about time they took off their rose-colored glasses and faced reality like mature, responsible adults.

I have said this, or something like it, so often to so many love-bedazzled young couples and seen them nod seriously but only half understand, that we now hold in our church (during the Sunday School hour) an eight-session series on preparation for marriage. At the end of it, I ask the young couples who have participated to submit unsigned evaluations.

I have received some excellent suggestions and helpful criticism. But the main thing is that, in one way or another, each of the couples say, "The best thing we have learned from this course is to be honest with each other about our feelings and to bring everything out in the open so we can talk about it."

One or two couples always come to see that they really aren't suited for each other and decide not to get married.

For those who are prepared to see, then, let's look at the three most important factors you can take into the "honorable estate."

Concept, Character, and Courage to Change.

We'll begin with the right concept of what a solid Christian marriage really is, and any marriage that begins without it is in for some real problems.

For Christians, marriage is *a sacred commitment to a permanent partnership.* It is not, as the New Morality would have it, just another contract between two parties which can be later broken off if things don't go as smoothly as planned. If it were merely a contract, lawyers on both sides would make sure there was an escape clause

37

in it, "in the eventuality of unforeseen difficulties arising, both parties shall have the option to cancel."

But there is no escape clause in "for better, for worse; for richer, for poorer; in sickness, in health." Not only does the marriage ceremony cover every eventuality in either direction, it requires the couple to pledge themselves to a lifetime commitment, "so long as ye both shall live." What's more, it requires this pledge to be made publicly, in the form of sacred vows before God and a whole congregation of witnesses, who, in turn, validate it by their participation. In fact, the permanence and public declaration of this unconditional commitment are part of what makes a Christian marriage a religious experience.

Obviously this can only be a summary definition of the basic concept of Christian marriage. The book, taken as a whole, offers a somewhat broader delineation, but the best advice I can give anyone prior to marriage is to sit down and talk over your respective concepts in detail. Make sure that the roles you expect each other to fill in your home are fully discussed and agreed upon well in advance of the wedding.

6

Character Counts

The second main factor in the making of a Christian marriage, and its most important single ingredient, is *character*—the relative strength of character (or lack of it) that you and your mate bring to the union.

By character I mean the whole outlook of his person—his maturity, his temperament, his ability to cope with stressful situations, how much he has died out to his selfishness, his ego, and so on. It may sound a bit old-fashioned to be referring to character, but the truth is, a marriage is no better than the material that goes into it. The person who has "the fruit of the Spirit—love, joy, peace, patience, kindness, goodness, faithfulness, gentleness, self-control" (Galatians 5:22, 23)—operating in his life is going to make a success of his marriage.

On the other hand, the carnal Christian who does not get along well with others and has been a continual problem to himself and his peers, is not likely to change just because he has gone through the marriage ceremony. How utterly naive many of us are to expect marriage to solve our inner problems and take care of our basic lack of character and spiritual depth. We are almost as naive as those who look to marriage as the panacea for all their problems—and discover they have merely exchanged one set of problems for another.

But there is an even greater folly in thinking that the thrill of the physical attraction between them is going to override all the defects of character. Exactly the opposite is the truth. Nothing can douse the flame of passion faster than selfishness, impatience, anger, or the inability to forgive. What then is love?

Since the greatest poets in history have yet to come up with a conclusive definition, it would be foolish for me to try. Fortunately, I don't need to. Paul did a pretty fair job in the first letter he wrote to the believers at Corinth (Chapter 13).

Love is patient. It suffereth long. Be careful about marrying someone who is very short on patience.

Love is kind. Is your partner a kind person?

Love is not jealous or envious. How often a young person comes to me about the problem of his partner's extreme jealousy! There's nothing wrong with a healthy concern, a desire to protect the one you love, and a strong feeling about anyone who would deliberately try to cut in on you. But there is a range of extreme jealousies far beyond that which is a clear warning signal of trouble ahead.

A young wife comes to me in great agony. Her husband is obsessed by jealousy and fiercely possessive, keeping her a veritable prisoner, accusing her of all kinds of affairs when there is no ground whatsoever. This isn't love; it's insanity.

Love is not proud or haughty. It is not selfish or rude; it doesn't demand its own way. Is your partner demanding? Or is he gracious and accommodating? Can he laugh at himself?

Love is not irritable or touchy. What temper can do within the framework of marriage is almost beyond belief. You'd be appalled at the infantile behavior some college graduates and even post-graduates are capable of, when their wills are crossed. If a child has never received proper discipline at the temper tantrum age, he is going to revert to that age when he gets severely crossed, no matter how many letters he may have behind his name.

What is it that can take two people so in love they can hardly talk and in a matter of months reduce their relationship to the point of physical violence? Carnal, uncontrolled anger!

We'll go into this in more depth in chapter 7, but let me ask one thing here: there is usually a split-second before the explosion, when you can choose not to express your anger. Do you? Or do you let 'er rip and inwardly enjoy it? How does your partner handle his anger?

Love does not keep account of evil. But what about being married to someone who does? What about the person who never forgets, who muddles every disagreement by reaching back into the past and dragging up some previous failure with which to club his partner over the head?

A girl came to see me about a problem she was having. Her fiance had "gone all the way" with a girlfriend in high school before he had become a Christian. He was a fine, deeply committed, and completely transformed young man now, and she had forgiven him, she assured me.

"But I just can't forget this. It keeps coming up and bothering me," she added.

I hear this from both sexes many times.

"If you can't forgive and forget, then you'd better find someone else. Either forget *it*, or forget *him*," I tell them.

To forgive and forget takes Christian character. It takes the kind of love Christ had at the cross. The Bible says in Ephesians 4:32, "And be kind to one another, tender-hearted forgiving each other, just as God in Christ also has forgiven you."

And God adds, "I will remember their sins no more" (Hebrews 8:12a).

Love "bears all things, believes all things, hopes all things, *endures all things*" (I Corinthians 13:7). Truly, this kind of love never fails. But this kind is more than natural human love; it is supernatural, divine love, as Romans 5:5

41

says, "The love of God has been poured out within our hearts through the Holy Spirit Who was given to us."

What all this means is: if there is anything in you that thinks of marriage as a kind of miracle drug for all your deficiencies, one that it will fill all your needs and answer all your problems, you are in for a rude awakening. You will be no better a marriage partner than you are a person, and neither will your fiance. But if you are the kind of Christian who gets along well with others, if your life manifests the fruit of the Spirit, then you have some of the best ingredients for a successful Christian marriage.

7

Growth Is the Watchword

The final major factor that is needed is the courage to change. *Growth* is the watchword here—like a great tree, a marriage keeps on growing and expanding as long as the couple continues to grow. The great hallmark of a Christian couple who are determined to have the best possible marriage is growth in understanding and love.

Growth—why is it so crucial? Because love is not static: it is dynamic. Like the true nature of the Christian life, it is a moment-by-moment process and cannot stand still. It is either going to grow larger, or it will grow smaller. And similarly, a husband and wife will either grow closer together, or they will grow further apart.

What happens as you grow together is that more and more *you learn to love your partner as he wants to be loved, not as you want to love.* This brings its own great reward, learning to live for the happiness of the other person and the surprising joy of doing so.

So, healthy growth depends upon death—the death of selfishness, of having to be right, of wanting one's own way, of living solely for one's self. As a tree must be pruned to bring forth fruit, a vine dressed, and a garden weeded, growth can be painful at times. It takes courage to face the pain; courage to change. But, isn't that what our lives on earth are all about? Are we not still here because there are still changes that God wants to work in us before He calls us home?

Ernest Hemingway once described courage as grace under stress, without, I suspect, knowing how true it was. As God the Husbandman prunes us in order that we might bring forth more fruit and thus be more conformed to His image, we need to pray for the grace to accept the change He would accomplish in us (John 15:1). With it, we have the courage and desire to die to our old natures, in order that we might come more alive in Christ than we dreamed possible. And conflict situations become new opportunities to grow, to choose His way over ours.

Growth and change. My wife Helen and I have discovered that as we grow, and especially as the children grow, everything keeps changing. When our older daughter left home, everything changed. Our second oldest became the eldest and everyone's relationships were topsy-turvy for awhile. Every move, every new place of work, every new school class brings about changes. Love has a thousand different faces and facets, and marriage requires the courage to continually change, to work out every new plateau of relationship into a new level of love.

"O God, who hast so consecrated the state of Matrimony that in it is represented the spiritual marriage and unity betwixt Christ and His Church; look mercifully upon these Thy servants, that they may love, honor, and cherish each other, and so live together in faithfulness and patience, in wisdom and true godliness, that their home may be a haven of blessing and of peace; through the same Jesus Christ our Lord, who liveth and reigneth with Thee and the Holy Spirit forever, one God, world without end."

8

Breaking the Heart of a Christian Marriage

Sermons on the problems of marriage often begin with the tired phrase, "And when the honeymoon is over . . ."

"Ted, is that our plane over there? The blue and white one?"

"Might be, I don't know. Now what did I do with them?"

"Well if it is, then why don't they process us through that gate over there, rather than making us walk all that way around. Ted, are you listening to me?"

"Honey, please. I'm trying to find our tickets. Maybe I put them in the camera case before. . . ."

"But you always used to listen to me before we were married. And we've only been married two days and six hours! Ted? Ted, never mind the tickets and listen to me!"

"Harriet, if I'd had any idea how much I was going to have to listen to you, we never would have *gotten* married!"

Sometimes the honeymoon is over almost before it's begun. There are many ways to tell when it's over. Someone has said that it is when the husband takes the wife off a pedestal and puts her on a budget. Dr. Paul Popenoe, the founder and president emeritus of the

American Institute of Family Relations, says it's over when both parties stop saying, "Darling you are absolutely perfect," and start saying, "You know, the trouble with you is . . ."

Another counselor sums it up by calling it the change from appreciation to depreciation.

As we examine the factors that tend to break the heart of a Christian marriage, it is not in a pessimistic or unromantic sense. On the contrary, we should have nothing but confidence and optimism, for the One who joined two of His followers together in holy matrimony is the grestest marriage counselor of all. What's more, He is always available, is fully apprised of our situation, possesses infinite wisdom and compassion, and really *cares* about us—even more than we do!

I know I haven't spoken too much about turning to Jesus Christ in time of need. Since this is a book primarily for Christians, I have merely assumed that His would be the *first* direction anyone would turn in, no matter what the problem. I mean, that is automatic in our Christian life, and if it isn't, it certainly should be. Thus every suggestion I make hereafter, as well as heretofore, should be read with the understanding that turning to God must be the first step in any solution.

The reason for going into the factors that cause marriages to break up is more than "to be forewarned is to be forearmed" and "an ounce of prevention is worth a pound of cure." Unless a marriage is grounded in reality—real people in real situations, letting God teach them to love each other as they really are—it has two strikes against it before it even comes to bat.

The opposite of reality is unreality. Many young people spend so much time in fantasyland it's no wonder there is such a loud noise when the honeymoon bubble finally bursts. The fellow looks upon his girl as though she were a goddess. She, in turn, exaggerates his every virtue into a glorious illusion. The truth is that they only partially see each other, and are looking at the part they do see through rose-colored glasses.

How could it be otherwise? Most of their contact has been at times of dating when each had his best foot forward, and these times alternate between times of desire and times of indifference. Romantic love concentrates on the times of desire and attraction and tends to ignore moments of indifference, difficulty, or actual aversion. *However, once you are married, it is necessary to incorporate even those negative experiences into your relationship.* And those difficult times are not to be just endured; they are to be woven into the very fabric of married life.

In addition to all this is the fact that before marriage your sexual desires are not being completely fulfilled, and this adds a sense of anticipation to further color every situation. After your marriage is consummated—and the Bible uses an interesting word for this: "And Adam *knew* Eve his wife" (Genesis 4:1, KJV)—there is literally nothing between you, and you know each other in the fullest sense of the word. In this knowing, the scales fall from your eyes, the rosy tint leaves your glasses, and you come to see one another as you really are. Gradually the period which has been called the time of mutual enjoyment of one another ends, and there begins the stage of mutual adjustment to one another. This has to be, because, as someone once said, "Two people wrapped up in each other make an awfully small parcel!"

As the picture changes from two young lovers facing each other, their hands joined, gazing lovingly into each other's eyes, to these same two, now side by side and hand in hand, with eyes forward on a common goal, what are some of the most perplexing problems during this period of adjustment? What are the ones which, if not faced honestly, could become so serious they could indeed break up a marriage?

9

How to Handle Money Problems

Four big problem areas face us engaged in marriage counseling. The first, surprisingly enough, is *finances*.

I say surprisingly, because while most people recognize that it's a problem area, they don't realize just how big it is. Interestingly enough, if affects the very rich as much as the very poor, and all the levels in between. The amount of money makes very little difference, because the problem is actually much deeper. The problem has to do with control or power or status, or, for that matter, restriction or humiliation or dependence versus independence.

Each partner comes into marriage with his or her own individual association with money, which comes from the background of his own home and his reaction to how his parents handled money. John R. Mott used to say that "money is minted personality," and he's right. Just as your own personalities are different, so your two minted personalities may be totally, even seemingly irreconcilably different.

When couples come to me for premarital counseling, they are usually surprised that I spend so much time talking about their financial plans and budget. Locally, we have a ready-made student situation which gives rise to many money problems, but it is a part of our whole American difficulty. With our tragic over-emphasis on sex, young people feel strong pressures which tend to push them into early marriages before they can afford to marry. And so we have many young married couples who are, as my grandmother vividly put it, "trying to live off the smell of a greased rag."

My suggestion to you is to put yourself on a budget as early in your married life as possible. It should be worked out carefully, prayerfully, and realistically. If you do so and stick to it, it is fair to say that you will avoid a great many marital problems and live within your means—no matter how little you might have. Unfortunately, the opposite is also true: if you don't have a budget, you will not live within your means, no matter how much money you might have.

Dr. David Mace makes a most helpful suggestion in his excellent book, *Success in Marriage.* Your budget should include small amounts for the husband and wife which are fully and freely their own and can be used by them in any way they desire—no questions asked by the other partner. This is a *must.* No husband can ever understand why in the world his wife bought that idiotic and useless "whatchamacallit," and no wife can ever quite fathom why her husband bought that ridiculous gadget for his camera. Never mind—don't try to understand; give each other perfect freedom in this, and you will both avoid some serious quarrels.

Communication is the second main problem area about which couples come for counseling, either for their inability to communicate or a breakdown in communication.

It is no great news that opposite personality patterns are often attracted to one another. We almost subconsciously reach out for a mate who will help us overcome our inadequacies by his particular strengths. The silent, reserved person is often drawn to a partner who is more outgoing and talkative. There is nothing

49

wrong with this, unless "the law of conjugal counter-balance," as Paul Tournier, the Swiss psychiatrist, calls it, goes into effect. Then, instead of complementing one another and helping one another, we drive each other into even greater extremes by our differences.

For example, we often find a quiet, impassive, and unexpressive husband with a talkative, expressive wife (though sometimes it is just the other way around). Before marriage, the young man enjoyed her talk; she was helping to bring him out, he said. After marriage, he had a different name for it: nagging.

I would like to add here that I can't blame some wives. Life with their husbands is like living with a great stuffed clam; they never share themselves, never talk about their work, or anything else, and they never have a word of appreciation or love. Sometimes wives come to me out of sheer desperation. They simply do not know what to do to reach their husbands, and in an effort to get through the invisible plastic shield and get any kind of response, they do the worst thing they could possibly do: they resort to nagging. This only succeeds in driving their husbands further into their shells.

Unfortunately, the American culture has put a positive emphasis on "the strong, silent type" as being masculine. Men are never supposed to show their emotions or let you know their feelings. But wives, I'll let you in on a secret: *deep down, a man is secretly wanting his wife to open up his heart, to help him find real emotional freedom.*

Very carefully, you must learn to possess your soul in patience and draw out of your husband his deepest feelings. This will not be easy; it will require great patience, but every woman is equipped to do this by her very femininity. She can create in the home a warmth and peaceful confidence which will help him do what he really wants to do: express himself and his love. If you do this, you will earn your husband's deep devotion and gratitude.

50

Men can be so obtuse sometimes. Their homes can be collapsing all around them and they will scarcely notice it. More than one wife has come weeping through my door, saying she can't stand it any longer. Her husband looks on in amazement, then turns to me with a blank expression and asks, "What problem? We don't have any problem."

From time to time I have advised a wife to write her husband a letter, telling him how much she really loves him, and then telling him frankly and openly some of the things that have been troubling her. Recently I advised a desperate wife to write her husband such a letter and mail it to him at his place of work. Very lovingly, but honestly and firmly, she laid it on the line.

He was so mad that for the first three days he said almost nothing. But she just prayed and poured on the unconditional, no-strings-attached love, though at times it was like trying to love a porcupine. Finally on the fourth day he broke down, admitted she was right, and told her he appreciated the fact that she hadn't nagged. Then he asked her to help him work on the problem. And she silently thanked God.

When communication goes, everything goes. Love, by its very nature, demands communication. Keep the lines open at any cost, even if it costs you your pride.

10

Damaged Emotions

The third potential marriage-breaker is *emotional immaturity.*

It is a sad thing that so many people marry in order to solve an emotional problem, because, as we have indicated, *marriage does not solve your personality problem, it only provides it a new arena in which to work* and will probably help increase it! The emotionally immature person is not going to suddenly grow up, just because he says those magic words at the altar. And the tragedy of life is that there are married men and women, twenty, thirty or fifty years old, who are certainly old enough to be married, but who have never begun to grow up in their emotions.

Such a person is still a child, whose life is characterized by sheer childishness, selfishness, temper tantrums, outbrusts, pouting, deep feelings of inferiority and insecurity, total irresponsibility, the inability to make even the simplest decision—the list is endless, and the results are tragic. Worst of all, so many of these same traits tend to be handed down from one generation to the next.

Wherever I go, I find this area of what I call our "damaged emotions" one of the neediest and yet most neglected in preaching and teaching.

If you are not yet married and you find this problem arising during courtship, I plead with you to go get help on it. Don't be so naive as to think it will go away or get better with time. It won't. It is so much easier to take care of *before* you get married; then it is only *your* problem. It is easier for the Lord, through a competent counselor, to get at the root of the problem for healing and deliverance. But after marriage, a whole new set of defenses and layers may cover it and make it much harder to change. So get help—now.

If you *are* married, you must have the courage to face problems in this area honestly. It takes courage to try to discover "the inner child of your past," to learn how to handle him and to "put away childish things." But don't be afraid; face up to your problems and *get help on them.*

There are many of us who have been brought up on the false teaching that the solution to every problem is a directly spiritual and strictly private one.

We've been told if we read our Bibles more and pray harder this is the way to solve everything. If we seek help from someone else we are admitting spiritual weakness. This is false and misleading. I have seen utterly miserable Christian couples drag on for years and years, unable to change some deeply neurotic pattern in their marriage, and failing to find victory because they were too spiritually proud to admit they needed help.

We have forgotten James 5:16a: *"Therefore, confess your sins to one another, and pray for one another, so that you may be healed."*

The fourth and final marriage-breaker is the *inability to resolve conflict.*

I tell many couples who come to me for help, *"Your difficulty is that you have never learned to fight like Christians!"* As we have seen, *conflict is not a dirty word;* great spiritual growth can come of it, and as we will see in the next chapter, *it is the price of growing intimacy.* In fact, every intimate human relationship includes it. The couple who say they never disagree or have conflict are either both liars or one of them is a vegetable!

It is not a question of having conflicts. The question is, how do you resolve them? In Christ, or in decibels? *The greatest crisis in marriage is discovering mature Christian ways of resolving differences and conflicts.* Some of the subtle and neurotic ways by which we try to win an argument or get our own way in the end are incredible.

The tragedy is that many couples don't even realize what is taking place. Everything is so varnished over with piety they are unconscious of the real motives, resentments and vindictiveness they are expressing. They would be shocked if anyone were to suggest that they were not above using emotional or spiritual blackmail.

Probably the most important ingredient in handling marital conflicts and hurts is the willingness and ability of "speaking the truth in love, we are to grow up in all aspects into Him . . . ." (Ephesians 4:15).

The trouble is, most of us so seldom speak the truth to one another that when we do, it comes in a blast of pent-up anger that could not by any stretch of imagination be likened to love. At which point, our opposite number either discounts the truth of what we have spoken as, "Oh well, he's just mad; he didn't really mean it," or retaliates with, "Well, you're being so terribly self-righteous, how do you expect me to hear anything you're saying?"

What we need is to make a habit of speaking the truth in love on a regular, continual basis. This is another way of saying that we should get what's bothering us out in the light so it can be dealt with in openness and honesty.

The alternative is to stuff it down on top of a lot of other things we've repressed, until we either explode, or start expressing our resentments *in*directly in a little back-stabbing put-down covered by laughter, or seemingly innocent physical slights, or any of the other weapons in our arsenal of dirty fighting, with which we get back at each other.

What if a little pain is involved to one's pride in order to accept a truth spoken in love? Isn't that a small price to pay for the peace and joy that come from living in the light? Would you really rather walk around miserable in darkness, making those around you miserable, too? A Christian family is too close-knit not to have all members affected by one's dark mood, even if nothing is said openly. *"If we say that we have fellowship with Him and yet walk in the darkness, we lie and do not practice the truth; but if we walk in the light as He Himself is in the light, we have fellowship with one another, and the blood of Jesus His Son cleanses us from all sin"* (I John 1:6, 7).

When it comes to conflict, the Bible is indeed the Manufacturer's Handbook. How little men have changed in 2,000 years! And how much help we can find there! The Phillips Paraphrase of Ephesians 4:26,27 says, "If you are angry, be sure that it is not out of wounded pride or bad temper. Never go to bed angry; don't give the devil that sort of foothold!" Ephesians 4:32 is another favorite of mine, both in my marriage and when I counsel others. "And be kind to one another, tender-hearted, forgiving each other, just as God in Christ also has forgiven you."

Standing at the foot of the cross of Christ together, both partners realize how much they have been forgiven by God. This makes it easier; *it gives them grace to forgive one another*—for Christ's sake.

Gradually this becomes not just one instance or a series of instances, but *the basic underlying attitude of both partners,* until they stop looking for perfection in one another and look for perfection only in God. They are in the process of becoming as loving and accepting and forgiving of one another as Christ has been toward them.

Several years ago I had a speaking engagement near Washington, D.C. My wife Helen was to take me to the airport in Lexington to catch the airplane.

I was fuming because I am a schedule-maniac and she was late. When we finally arrived at the boarding-gate, the attendant stopped us.

55

"I'm sorry, but we've taken your name off the list."

We had a bit of discussion, after which he said he could guarantee me a seat only as far as Charleston. I was angry.

When I arrived in Charleston, it turned out there was plenty of room. Between Charleston and Washington, the Holy Spirit began to deal with me. By the time we landed, my heart was changed. I went straight to the newsstand, got a postcard and wrote Helen:

"I'm sorry."

When I arrived at the church where I was scheduled to preach, there was a call from Helen.

"I'm so sorry I made you late," she said.

That was it; it was all over. Now I could preach with the peace of a clear conscience.

"Forgiving each other, just as God in Christ also has forgiven you . . ." (Ephesians 4:32). We need to cultivate this ability to resolve our conflicts *in the love of God,* for only in His love is there sufficient love to meet every need in marriage. There are times when the cup of human love can run low; it can even seem to go completely dry. That's when we must hold our cups up to God's great Niagara of divine love, and ask Him to refill them. *When we give Him our willingness to love, He always gives us the power to love.* His supernatural love restores our natural love.

11

The Price of Intimacy

Early in the Bible we find God's description of an ideal marriage. "For this cause a man shall leave his father and his mother, and shall cleave to his wife; and they shall become one flesh" (Genesis 2:24).

"Yes," there is always someone who asks, "but *which* one?"

There are at least two things in the world that prove conclusively that God has a sense of humor; the second is the duck-billed platypus.

The first is marriage, and if you don't have the sense of humor to see that, then you'd better pray for one; you're going to need it. Marriage is the most impossible, inconceivable, unutterable—fantastic institution on the face of this earth!

I don't think it was any accident that Jesus happened to perform his first miracle while at the wedding feast in Cana where he changed the water into wine, for it takes a miraculous tranformation of divine love and grace if the daily messy-sink, messy-desk realities of married life are to be turned into elements of joy.

The messiest reality of all is unresolved conflict. We Christians have been slow to face the fact that conflict is the price of growing intimacy and love between two persons.

This is as true of your relationship with God, or a friend, as with your marriage partner. We have especially failed to face up to our negative feelings in marriage. Many of us have destroyed our relationships because, in a very *un*scriptural manner, we have steadfastly refused to face honestly our real feelings about one another. We have been brainwashed by "happy-face Christianity," which demands a great big smile for every circumstance. There can never be any conflict; negative feelings and every surface disturbance are to be hushed and calmed.

Quite the contrary the Bible knows perfectly well we're going to have conflict. We are all forgiven sinners, aren't we? As we saw in the previous chapter, Paul has made a number of specifically helpful suggestions on how, when and where to resolve marital conflict. So did Peter, who had one advantage over Paul: he knew marriage from firsthand experience.

Have you thought about Peter as a married man? In the Gospels, we're told that Jesus healed Peter's mother-in-law. Knowing Peter, he must have loved both his wife and her mother dearly. And knowing how impulsive and stubborn the Big Fisherman could be, if he had a wife at all worth her salt, I suspect they probably had a conflict or two. Have you ever seen a good, strong marriage without them? I haven't.

How do you suppose he resolved them? I imagine that, before he met his Master, it was not that rare to hear raised voices in his household: Peter was too blunt, too much of a blurter, to repress anything for very long. He would want it expressed and out in the open.

But then read I Peter 3:1-17, and see what an extraordinary change has been worked in him, after three years of doing it Jesus' way under the tutelage of the Holy Spirit. What a beautifully tender, meek-hearted attitude towards husband and towards wife! If that amount of change can be worked in such a man in such a comparatively short time, isn't there hope for every one of us?

How did the Peter who wrote that letter resolve conflict? With humility. Willing to be the wrong one, the greater sinner. Willing to hear the truth spoken to him, even if it wasn't delivered lovingly. In fact, grateful for it *any* way it came, that he might see another area where he could become more like his beloved Master. Not making excuses for himself nor looking at any sin in the speaker that could be used as an excuse not to listen.

And if it were given to Peter by the Holy Spirit to speak a certain truth to another, how did he do that? From a lowly position, having first gone to God with the beam in his own eye, with compassion, knowing full well that another beam could easily be in his own eye again tomorrow. And always with love—love that cared enough to free a brother or sister in Christ from a sin they were blind to, even at the risk of incurring enmity. Tough love.

If somewhere in the process, it turned out that Peter was not yet perfectly conformed to Christ's image, if self began to come in, he confessed it, asking the Lord to forgive him and change his heart. Then he went on. A relationship that was probably strong before was stronger than ever afterward.

That's the model. We must do likewise.

Would that it were so easy! Look, you're going to make mistakes; you might as well resign yourself to that right now. Somebody is going to be speaking truth to you, and sooner or later, you're going to blow, rather than choosing to hang in there and silently plead to Jesus to help you hear what's being said to you.

But just because you blow it occasionally, just because you're not perfect, *don't* let that stop you and your mate from trying to live in the light with one another. Even if at first you seem to fall back two steps for every three forward, those few steps forward are going to make a world of difference. Wait and see.

Jesus said, "I am the way, and the truth, and the life" (John 14:6). We already know He's the way. What we're talking about here is the truth—the truth which sets us free from the bondage of our old sinful nature. And what lies ahead is the life—life in Christ, in openness and honesty with one another, life of sustained joy and peace such as we've never experienced before, though many of us had a foretaste of it at the time of conversion.

We need help in seeing where we need to change. Let's look at some of the areas where many of us need help and may not realize it.

I would like to borrow an idea from George Bernard Shaw, who said that ever since Adam allowed weeds to grow in the Garden of Eden, man has allowed weeds in his life that threaten his survival. The same is true of the weeds in the garden of marriage: if you let them run loose, they can threaten its very survival.

12

Love and Grow

Let's begin with the idea that the marriage garden is a place where *love* is intended to *grow*. "Love" and "grow" are the two important words. We've already seen the need for growth in our lives; now we will take a closer look at love, specifically the different kinds of love. C.S. Lewis said there are four, and a happy marriage is made up of a balance of all four.

First, there is *need love*.

This is the basic hunger to *be* loved, to be needed and wanted, to belong to someone. This kind of love was acknowledged by God in the beginning: "it is not good for the man to be alone" (Genesis 2:18a).

All of us need to be needed. We want to be wanted. In fact, some people's motto is, "It's better to be wanted for murder than not to be wanted at all." And they do some pretty horrendous things to satisfy their "need love."

There has to be *some* "need love" on both sides in marriage—but the love-starved person who reaches out for any arms he or she can find makes an impossible partner, because of this unquenchable thirst.

You can't be happily married to someone else until you are first happily married to yourself. Otherwise, you will marry out of emptiness and deep insecurity, and "need love" that is too demanding will destroy the very relationship it is trying to establish.

Then there is *eros*—biological, sexual love.

Married love definitely includes its fullest physical expression, and is intended to be filled with joy and ecstasy. When Paul counsels Corinthian couples (I Corinthians 7:3-5) that marriage partners have rights over each other's bodies and are not to abstain from sexual expression except by mutual consent for an agreed-upon time in order to wholly concentrate on spiritual devotion, after which they are to resume relations, he is plainly implying that eros love is for purposes other than procreation. Eros love is part of the divine design. It is the physical, sacramental expression of the one-flesh relationship.

Third comes *philia love*—comradeship, companionship, friendship.

This, too, was acknowledged in God's providing Adam a helpmate, a partner to share with. How much more fun it would have been to have someone with whom to talk over the names he had picked for all the animals! Sharing, day in and day out, is absolutely essential in any marriage and grows even more so as the marriage matures.

Finally, there is *agape,* the love which comes directly from God Himself.

This is the divine love that enables a human to accept another human exactly as he is, the love that can forget as well as forgive, the love that knows no limits or end, the highest form of love.

God created "need love." He created "eros love." He created "philia love." But He did not create "agape love," for He is Himself agape love. Therefore, "agape love" is not indigenous; it is not natural to the created order of things. It has to come from outside the order. It is not something that can be developed by human effort.

"I'll love her if it *kills* me!" an irate husband exclaims.

"It's likely to kill both of you in the process!" is my reply.

"Agape love" is a gift. It is God-given, supernatural, redemptive, healing unconditional love. It is covenant love, commitment love, surrender love—love that is based on the will and does not depend on the emotions. Agape love comes only from God.

There is a balance of these four loves growing together in the garden of marriage. But there are also weeds—some terrible, virulent species which can stunt or stifle or completely stop the growth of love. Then the garden becomes a veritable jungle—a mass of feelings and attitudes and actions that can take over and utterly ruin it.

Let me share from pastoral experience a few of the most common, home-grown, garden variety weeds.

The first is the deadly *turned-head weed.*

This one grows in one direction, but the head faces in the opposite direction. You might call it the "if only" weed. It makes a peculiar noise when the wind blows through it. It whines, "Look what I've given up to marry you." Or, "If only I had married Freddie when he asked me." This weed lives on the memories of bygone days, of former loves, of past opportunities. It lives in a fantasy world of the past which it keeps reinforcing with old memories, old snapshots that should have been burned a long time ago. A letter in the basement which you only look at once in awhile . . .

Scores of movies and dramas have been written about this weed: about the husband or wife who hangs onto an old fantasy of the past, an old boyfriend, a might-have-been person. Such a person goes through life system-atically destroying his present marriage, his partner and children until all is in shambles.

Often towards the end the clever novelist or dramatist brings you to the horrible moment of disillusionment, when our fantasist actually meets the real it-might-have-been person she has dreamed about all these years—only to discover that he is no longer tall, dark and handsome but fat, bald and ugly—and obnoxious, to boot.

The shock is all the more magnified by the years of unreal fantasy. The truth is he never *was* quite that tall or dark or handsome. Thus, life imitates art, only the sad thing is, in life the moment of truth often comes too late and sometimes never comes at all.

A woman who had been married seventeen years came to see me. Her marriage was almost on the rocks, and after a few conversations I could see what her problem was. One day, in one of those beautiful moments when the Holy Spirit does what you can't do she saw it. With a stunned expression on her face, she said to me, "I can't believe it. For seventeen years I've been living out of a suitcase."

"What do you mean?"

"You know," she said, shaking her head slowly, "I've never unpacked my bags, I've never settled down, committed myself to my husband and family. All these years I've been doing slow motion video replays of things in the past. It's all been a mirage, and I've been living in it."

Have you?

By commitment, the Bible means that you say yes to one, and no to everyone else. Mentally unpack your bag and make the commitment; this is the way you get rid of this patch of weeds in your garden.

But it takes drastic action. Don't just cut off the the top of the "turned-head weed," or it will grow back again, bigger than ever. You've got to get down to the roots, to dig up and throw away some things. There are some doors in your life that need to be slammed and locked and bolted, some things that need to be destroyed and burned and put away.

Then begin thanking God for your marriage partner. (When did you last thank Him for him or her? Has it been a long time? Too long?)

Thank God for what you've gained, not lost. You've gained an opportunity to share your joys and sorrows with another person. You have someone to love you and to belong to, to stand by you in sickness and in health. Someone *real,* not a fantasy image on your secret late show. Every day thank God for the one He has given you. And that noxious, "turned-head weed" will wither and die.

Next, we come to the *I-me weed.*

This hardy specimen grows to enormous heights, till you can't see anything else in the garden. Its name comes from two ancient English words, *I* and *me,* that derive from the same root: *mine,* one of the earliest words a child learns.

This weed is a real love-choker! It throttles marriages, turns homes into thickets of in-fighting and competition. The exact opposite of selfless "agape love," this weed quickly makes itself the center of the marriage garden.

"*I* am the most important person! What do *I* get out of it? No, *I* don't care what you've planned, *I* don't want to go there . . ." Some of the favorite expressions of the I-me weed are: "My money, my house, my kids, my car, my folks, and my plans." Unless great care is exercised—and this weed is exorcised—you may wind up with "my divorce."

The best way to get rid of the I-me weed is to sow the seed of the *our-we* plant. Talk, dream, plan for *our* and we. This helps us to think in terms of *our* money, *our* house, *our* car, *our* folks and *our* plans. And it is so basic, for, as the Bible says, the two *shall* become one. Two I's are now turned into one *we;* two *mines* are turned into one *ours.*

Let's for a moment call an earth-moving implement a spade: the I-me weed is a fancy name for plain selfishness. Is it choking the good plants in your garden to death?

Then there's the *clam-up* weed.

This is an insidious pest—not one of the lushest but one of the toughest to get to the root of. Because when one party "clams up," he makes it almost impossible for the other to find out why.

"What's wrong, honey?"

Silence.

"Is it something I said?"

The silence of the clam is like unto the silence of the tomb.

"Is it something I didn't say?"

A sigh. Perhaps a little groan. More silence.

This, as we have seen in the previous chapter, is the dirtiest kind of fighting, because there's no recourse. When this deadly weed takes over, a hush falls over the marriage garden. Silence settles in as repression of deep feelings takes place. Sometimes years go by; things get pushed down and held down. And then one day, the volcano erupts. Suddenly there is a separation and everyone is shocked.

In 1972, the divorce statistics for our country showed an interesting change. If you were to make a chart of the years from one to twenty-five in marriage, the peaks for divorce are the third and fourth years. Then it levels off, until suddenly in the seventeenth, eighteenth, and nineteenth years there comes another sharp rise as veteran married couples break up. The statistics are borne out; we can see it happening among Christians in our churches, everywhere. Why this great tragedy? Mainly because the "clam-up" weed has had all those years to entrench itself, till finally there's a cataclysmic explosion and the marriage garden is destroyed.

The last weed we'll look at is the *wandering affection weed.*

It's small and ugly and its leaves are very sharp. So are its roots: they cut the roots of love under the surface, out of sight, so that love doesn't even know what's happening. Under certain conditions it can be the fastest-growing weed in the garden.

Some of us let this weed get started because we hold onto the myth that when you get married you'll never be attracted to another person again. Ridiculous! Just because you love a person, deeply love him or her, doesn't mean that you lose your power to be attracted to someone else. The circumstances of our society actually encourage this, what with men and women working together in different places. The loosely-knit home life weakens the bond between many couples.

In my office, I have seen people shocked to realize that they are gripped by a strong attraction for "someone else." They never thought it was possible that Christians could have this happen to them. They are plagued with deep guilt.

True marital love has its basis in the will, not the emotions. The fact that you get married doesn't make you automatically immune to temptation. It doesn't change your basic humanity, your masculinity or femininity. It does mean you have made a fundamental choice, a commitment of the will to belong to another "till death do us part."

How do you get rid of the wandering affection weed? First, try to nip it in the bud. That's so important! Don't let the little devil get started, because it grows so quickly! In almost no time at all, the wandering glance can become the lustful look. The open sharing and companionship can soon become something deeper. We married Christians really need the antiseptic power of the Holy Spirit surrounding us, to cleanse and purify us in our relationships, the casual ones as well as the more serious.

I've heard it with such sadness—"It began when we were praying together. We became close friends. Suddenly, before we knew it, we were in each other's arms . . ."

Nip it in the bud! That's number one.

But what if you are already in the grip of this dilemma? You feel dry and empty and utterly feelingless towards your married partner. What should you do?

Make a list of everything your wife or husband really likes. Actually sit down and write out a list. Then go out and *do* these things for your husband or wife!

Keep in mind that I Corinthians 13—that great description of agape love—says not a word about feelings. It doesn't say anything about them, because *real love is a way of behaving.*

So go and *do* the loving thing for your partner, and keep on doing it. Ask the Lord to change your feelings. Don't worry, if you're obedient, they'll soon fall into line.

William James was a psychologist years ahead of his time. He said, "If you go through the proper motions, the desired emotions are bound to follow." E. Stanley Jones put it another way, equally good. At times, he said, we have to "act ourselves into a new way of feeling, in order to feel ourselves into a new way of acting."

So *do* the loving thing. I give this prescription, and the confused husband goes out the door. In two or three weeks (it never takes longer than that) he's back. He says, "Doc, we're on a second honeymoon!"

What happened? "Agape love" came in and refilled the cup of marriage. Natural love was dry and needed to be replenished by His supernatural love.

Is your cup dry? Is the wine of joy, romance and happiness in your marriage running low? Don't look for another cup; remember the wedding feast in Cana, and take your empty cup to Jesus.

"Fill it with water," He said. Sometimes that means tears of repentance, the "I'm sorry, honey," the fresh sharing together. It takes a few tears. But He will soon turn the water into the wine of joy and love.

13

The Spirit of Forgiveness

The prize for the most ridiculous single line ever uttered in a ridiculous movie has got to go to "Love Story" for the line that attracted all the attention: "Love means never having to say you're sorry."

Love *is* saying, "I'm sorry. Please forgive me."

Love is the putting down of pride to say it, the being willing to be the first to say it, and the tearful repentance from which the words spring.

We have seen that the ability to resolve conflict is the single most important factor in the making of a Christian marriage. And, we have also seen that the spirit of forgiveness is the key to that ability, and that it can be cultivated until it becomes *the basic underlying attitude of both partners.* Now is the time to take a good look at this beautiful, tender flower and see how it grows.

One reason why there is such a need for the spirit of forgiveness is so obvious that it's often disregarded: the basic differences between a man and a woman. Actually they're just barely the same species!

It doesn't take long after marriage for some of the more subtle differences to cause tremendous misunderstandings.

For example, take basal metabolism. It's almost

inevitable that two opposites will disagree on this. I like to get up early, go to bed early. When I wake up, I'm wide awake and ready to go. But my wife Helen is just the opposite. She's not even civil until after her second cup of coffee. She's pooped out by late afternoon, but then she gets her second wind around 11 or 12 o'clock at night. I've never seen anyone who could get so much done between midnight and when she finally goes to bed, and needless to say, sometimes it has given rise to conflict.

On the other hand, I am, as I've already mentioned, a punctuality nut, but my wife is totally unconcerned. For years, when our family was going anywhere, my way of helping was to get in the car and honk the horn periodically until the others came out. One day she cured me of this. She said, "Honey, I'll tell you what. Let's *you* take care of getting the kids ready, and I'll sit in the car and honk the horn."

Then there's the matter of the inner thermostat which, I guess, is also tied in with metabolism: we are exactly the opposite.

I'm very warm-blooded and need only a light blanket to sleep under. Helen, however, can be freezing under a mountain of blankets. And so we have an almost daily ritual. I come into the house, take off my coat.

"Did you turn up the thermostat?"

She comes in, puts on an angora sweater and says, "Did you turn down the thermostat?"

In all honesty, one of the things that has saved our marriage is an electric blanket with dual controls. One of the most horrible nights we can ever remember was when we somehow got those controls switched. I kept turning mine lower and freezing her, while she kept turning hers up so that by morning I felt like I'd been poached.

These little-big differences—and they come as small as you want to get—are what may have caused the man celebrating his twenty-fifth anniversary to ponder a moment before replying to the question, "Have you ever seriously considered divorce?"

"Divorce never," he replied, "but murder often."

Once a couple decided to get wall-to-wall carpeting. In order to save money the husband spent one evening laying the carpet himself. He worked with great care and effort. At length he was finished and straightened up to survey his handiwork, at which time he decided he'd have a smoke. He felt all his pockets and looked around for his cigarettes but they were nowhere to be found. Just about that time, he noticed a lump under the carpet, in one corner.

Oh, brother, did his heart fall! But he was not about to take up all that carpeting and do it over again. So he just went over to the lump and ground it under his foot—putting all his weight on it until only a slight tumor was noticeable.

He tiptoed into the kitchen where his wife was fixing him a snack.

"Well, even if I did it, it looks pretty good. There is one little uneven spot over in the corner by the window, but you were going to put the green chair there anyhow, so no one will notice it."

He ate the snack, patted his shirt pocket without thinking.

"Say, you haven't seen my cigarettes, have you?"

"Sure, they're right here on the windowsill. By the way, have you seen the parakeet?"

Let's face it: in the best of marriages, there's a parakeet under the rug somewhere. I know you're thinking that the one under yours is as big as a buzzard. But the point is, we're all so human! We're so sinful! We fail in so many ways! We all need the spirit of forgiveness, as much of it as we can get!

Right off the bat in marriage, both partners are going to need the spirit of forgiveness in abundance. They didn't know they were going to have conflicts. (As I've indicated, I find this almost impossible to communicate to the semi-conscious young lovers who come to my office for premarital counseling.) Then they get married, and it's a while before they discover that their partner is not deliberately trying to be mean or nasty or stubborn—he or she is just being himself. There's a lot of conflict involved in finding this out, and there also needs to be an equal amount of forgiveness to go with it.

14

Resentment

Every couple needs to fall in love twice—at least twice. The first time, you fall in love and get married—and then you find out that your divine mate is pretty human after all, and that you've been asking a human mate to do and be what only a perfect God can do and be.

So the second time you fall in love, you don't fall into it; you *climb* into it. This time you love the real person, not the fantasy person on whom you first projected the imaginary qualities of Sleeping Beauty or Prince Charming.

Someone has said that the real problem in marriage is not to *find* the right person but to *be* the right person.

Andre Maurois says much the same thing: "I have chosen. From now on my aim will not be to search for someone who will please me, but to please the one I have chosen."

Many people waste years of married life looking for an imaginary partner or trying to change the real partner, instead of learning to live with and love the real partner they actually married. Some of us are like marital Michelangelos. With hammer and chisel we sculpt away, trying to change our partners into the person we thought we were marrying, the person we want him or her to be.

Louise Moore has a good word on this: "For twenty years I prayed this prayer, 'Lord, you love my husband, while I change him.' For twenty years he was an alcoholic. One day God said to me, 'Louise, you've got our roles mixed up. You love him and let Me change him.' "

She did—and within two years he was converted.

The greatest lesson I learned in the Asbury College revival of 1970 was that God had not called me to change anyone; He had only called me to love people. When we love, it's marvelous how people change! But it has to begin with us.

The instinctive thing is to wait for your partner to make the first move; to wait till he changes enough to suit you. All the time you are thinking, *If only she would do this or do that, if only, if only, if only.* But the Bible says you've got to take the initiative. God's "agape love" takes the initiative. He never waited for you or me to change before He started loving us. "While we were yet sinners, Christ died for us" (Romans 5:5b).

I've said before that mature love is learning how to love your partner in the way he or she wants to be loved, not in the way you *think* he or she wants to be loved, because that's the way *you* want to love.

What I didn't say was that it took me ten years to realize that one of the ways Helen likes to say, "I love you, David," is through her cooking.

Sometimes God speaks to her, and she sees some area where she needs some change, and she expresses her repentance and love by cooking some new, tasty, exotic recipe for me. You'd be amazed at some of the stuff I've eaten for the last thirty years!

But for ten years I was so dense that I didn't get it, because I wanted love in a certain way.

I particularly remember two missionaries whose marriage was in deep trouble. After talking with them a short time, I realized that, while they had been married seventeen years they had never really faced each other as they really were. She had married him thinking that

74

because he was going to be a missionary, he must be quite spiritually advanced and had assumed he would provide the spiritual leadership, discipline and standards in the family. She had hoped he would be all that she wasn't, that he would be able to help her become what she was unable to be in her own strength.

Imagine her disillusionment when she discovered that he didn't have regular devotions, that he was sloppy and indisciplined in his Christian habits.

His disillusionment, it turned out, was just as acute. She had seemed to be such a sharp person, well groomed, neat, very feminine—he thought she would be an ideal wife and mother. Imagine his dismay when he discovered that all this was a mask of selfishness, that it was done for herself and the sake of her appearance. He couldn't stand the way she kept the house or cooked the food or looked after the kids—or rather, the way she *didn't* do these things. He said he could not feel warm and responsive towards anyone who was so irresponsible in the home.

Of course, each had suggested that the other should change. They had spent seventeen years saying this to each other in all sorts of ways—sculpting on one another, so to speak. They were convinced that if only the *other* would change, their marriage would be okay.

It became okay only after they realized what they were doing. Under God, they faced their deep failures in repentance and confession. The spirit of forgiveness took over, and God created a new love for each other—for the real person whom they had married, and for whom they were spiritually responsible. They learned real love, and on this foundation they built a truly Christian marriage.

15

Don't Use a Club

Although forgiveness is a wonderful ingredient, it must never become a weapon. It can be used as a means of emotional and spiritual blackmail to manipulate and control the partner, to put him or her into a spiritual and emotional squeeze, to use as a way of escaping some real problems that need to be faced. Some are always blaming the other person, demanding that he or she always ask for forgiveness, and condemning him unless he does.

There are many ways of forcing your marriage partner to say, "I'm sorry, please forgive me." I've spent hours with wonderful Christian men and women, trying to help them to change, telling them that what they're doing is not Christian but neurotic, and that it is destroying them as well as their partners.

What is forgiveness, anyhow?

Is it dismissing something lightly, and saying, "Oh, that's okay," when deep down you are hurting badly, and things are *not* okay?

No. Real forgiveness does not preclude speaking the truth in love. It's not covering over some real wrong, failing to treat it seriously. That's not love; that's apathy.

Real forgiveness is not cheap and easy. Real forgiveness is always more than mere understanding, more than mere acceptance. There is always a mutual sharing of the hurt and a facing of your true feelings before you can genuinely forgive the person who has wronged you. He must also feel his wrong and be in a spirit of true repentance before you can truly forgive him.

Forgiving is not just something people decide to give or receive in order to escape, in order to smooth things over, in order to put a quick band-aid on a deep wound, or as a balm to a guilty conscience.

Forgiveness is *not* peace at any price! In the long run that can produce deep resentment even between some very religious people. And then, repressed for thirty years, one day the lid finally blows off and everyone acts so surprised.

When Paul says be angry but do not sin, and get that anger taken care of before you go to bed, he is speaking to reality, for in reality there may well be times when you are very angry at your mate. We evangelical Christians have never differentiated between anger and hate, and it's one of our most costly mistakes. We need to see the distinction in our understanding of the anger and wrath of God, and in our relationships with our mates and our children.

A parent can be angry at a willfully disobedient child, but hate him? Hardly! Open anger is still wrong, but it is infinitely preferable to the hidden variety, which is not dealt with and which soon starts leaking out in vindictiveness.

What Paul is saying is that the *duration* of anger is important; it should be given up as soon as possible. This is facilitated by a quick prayer to the Lord, confessing the anger and asking Him to change one's heart, and to show one the reason for the anger. Then see whether the anger doesn't proceed from an unassailably right position that has just been assailed, or a bruised ego, or a stuffed-down hurt, or guilt, or a will that is crossed in an area where it shouldn't matter nearly as much as it obviously does, or as a diversionary tactic to keep from having to accept some unacceptable truth about oneself, or . . .

77

The list is endless, but the Holy Spirit is quick to point out the right cause, if He is asked to.

It is important to get the anger dealt with and under the blood of Jesus, because if it is allowed to persist or go underground, it can easily turn into resentment. And resentment, if allowed to ferment, becomes bitterness.

There are roughly four stages in a marital conflict. The first is the *wounded heart.*

It may be accidental or subconscious or semiconscious or quite conscious. (I'm afraid I've done it all those ways—and you have, too.) Paul says in Ephesians 4:32 in a verse which is the summation of the spirit of forgiveness: "Be kind to one another, tender-hearted." This means to be sufficiently sensitive to know when you have hurt your partner.

The Holy Spirit (sometimes with the very able assistance of my wife) has a wonderful way of making me know when I've hurt her. Suppose she has tried to tell me something, but I was sure I was right. Later, when I try to pray about it, God refuses to hear my prayers.

"If you won't listen to Helen, how are you going to listen to Me?" He says. "I've already spoken to you through her. Listen to her."

If we won't listen to the one we do see, we'll never hear the One we can't see.

If I'm tenderhearted, I would know in my heart that I had wounded Helen, and take care of it right away. But imperfect sinner that I am, I don't always do that—sometimes because I'm so busy serving the Lord in other places.

Let's face it: if you're a minister or a missionary or whatever, and you're *that* busy, then you're *too* busy!

The second stage is the *cold heart* (mine).

Now I don't feel it so much. I get *really* busy. Or perhaps I get extra nice to her. Isn't it interesting, the guilt-compensating mechanisms in a marriage? I volunteer to do the dishes, I get real helpful. But that isn't the issue.

In the meantime, my heart is getting colder. I want to do something about it, but it's much more difficult. I can feel the relationship getting colder, I can feel marital drift setting in. At this stage we often add other hurts. Things pile up, we go back and drag out older, former weapons to use.

If the Holy Spirit doesn't get us out of that stage, then we go into the third one: the *hard heart*.

Now I am defending. I am rationalizing. At the same time, God is getting into the act. He is working, the Spirit is prodding, but it is not going to be easy because I've waited so long. My heart is rapidly hardening.

Screwtape gets into the act now. He improves my eyesight, giving me 20-20 vision so I see every one of her faults in technicolor. I remember some other time like this that I was hurt in the past. Oh, yes, I'd forgiven that a long time ago, but under Screwtape's supervision my mind seems to do a video replay of that episode, only this time it's in slow motion.

Intimacy produces not only deepening love, but deeper risk of vulnerability. Thirty years has shown us all of each other's weakest salients, where we could really rip each other open. That's why Paul sternly warns, "Let all bitterness and wrath and anger and clamor and slander be put away from you, along with all malice" (Ephesians 4:31).

In this stage I can grieve the Holy Spirit out of my life, and if I persist in it, ancient temptations can arise, old scars, damaged emotions. Past victories can be undone. It's like the water level in the lake getting lower and lower during an especially dry year. Pretty soon all those old stumps reappear—junk and trash that's been covered by the beautiful lake for years. My prayers are hindered, as Peter, the married man, warned in his epistle. In fact, if the truth be known, I don't feel much like praying at all.

I've never gone past this stage, thank God. But there is a fourth stage: the *apathetic heart*.

That's when one or both partners come and say, "Pastor, I don't care. I don't give a hang what happens."

I have seen situations where marriage partners didn't seem to care that husband or wife was having an affair. The adultery, as hurtful as it should have been, didn't hurt as much as the other partner's not showing any hurt or anger.

"And you know, Pastor," the guilty partner would say, "I don't think she really does care!"

If they come to me and say, "I tell you, I can't stand him! I hate it," that's hopeful. But when people say "I just don't care anymore," then I know we're in for real trouble. For then God has to restore feeling. If feelings are gone, there's no resentment, because there's no pain, and there's no pain because there's nothing there to feel it.

16

The Answer

What's the answer? The place where we go to find the answer to every sin—personal, marital or social: "Just as God in Christ also has forgiven you" (Ephesians 4:32b). The answer is in the cross of Jesus Christ.

First, *stand beneath the cross.* Contemplate the cross. The highest Christian ethic is not, "Do unto others as you would have them do unto you." It is: *Do unto others as God has done unto you!* Stand beneath the cross. Do what God has done there for you. Find His fresh forgiveness. It won't be easy, but it will make forgiving your partner possible. Ask and receive forgiveness, the spirit of it, from the cross.

Second, *give God your will.* By your will I mean your willingness to forgive. Feelings may not change for awhile. That's not important. It's the *will* to forgive that's important. If you give God your willingness, He will ultimately change your feelings.

So many of us go wrong here. We mistake our feelings as the final judge. They aren't. If you obey God, He will take care of the feelings. Your job is to straighten out wrong relations. His job is to straighten up wrong feelings. Don't get your part and His part confused.

A wife shared with me that after praying, her prayers

were answered and her erring husband was restored to her. But her hurt—and the rancor it engendered—were still there. One day she read Phillips' paraphrase of I Corinthians 13: "Love does not keep account of evil."

The Holy Spirit said to her, "What about those letters in the bottom of the drawer?"

It was quite a battle, but she went to the drawer and took out a sheaf of letters, costly evidence against her husband, which she had been keeping for a long time. They had lain in that dismal drawer and soured her heart for years.

God had forgiven him his sins; she had *said* that she forgave him also. But she had kept the letters, the ultimate weapon. Now God had spoken, and so she burned them.

"At first I was panicky," she said, "when I saw the evidence going up in smoke. They were my last chance of ever getting even with him. Then a great peace came over me. And within a matter of days, a great flood of true love for my husband came."

She obeyed. She forgave. And she was blessed.

Third, *communicate your forgiveness, or your need for forgiveness, to your partner.*

That's hard, but you must break through. If you can't say it, and some people just can't seem to, then write it. Don't be afraid. Many a time I've advised a husband or wife to write a letter, so that their partner will get it alone. There is an awful silence sometimes, lasting two or three days, which is agony to endure. Then finally the partner will say, "I got your letter." And everything gets straightened out. But however you decide to do it, communicate!

Fourth, if there is an immediate full and free response, fine. Then *pray together*—and find new love restored in Christ. Most often this is what happens, but sometimes not. If not, don't push your partner; that's spiritual blackmail.

I know of a situation where one partner asked the other for forgiveness. There was a long silence. "Give me a little time, please. I can't quite say it yet," came the reply.

Instantly that partner who had asked for forgiveness felt hurt and disappointed. But the counteraction of the Holy Spirit was right there.

"Keep still!" He said. *"Let it go at that. And leave it alone."*

It wasn't long before the Holy Spirit gave both the will and the feelings for the other. Within days they were in each other's arms, weeping and praying, loving one another more deeply and honestly than they had ever dreamed possible.

After you've done your part, surrender it to God. Let God be God; don't try to play God for your mate.

Finally, *forgive yourself.*

We humans are so strange. We can take God's grace and misuse it in so many ways. We can even scourge ourselves for a long time and refuse to accept God's forgiveness. We can go through life doing what A.W. Tozer so beautifully called "the penance of perpetual regret."

I'm going to close this chapter with a deeply personal account out of the Kilbourne family, those great missionaries to Korea and Japan.

It was Friday afternoon, and Erny Kilbourne was speaking on the West Coast. His wife, Vi, was at home with the children, and there were teen-age problems. She was upset. She needed the father, the husband; she needed counsel. She was so distraught that in the middle of the afternoon, she called Erny in California.

What she didn't know was that he was in a meeting, on the platform, when they called him out to answer the telephone. When he answered, he was annoyed.

"They're waiting in there for me to speak," he said.

She tried to pour out her problem, but Erny was short with her. It was not a successful phone call.

Erny didn't sleep too well that night and by early the next morning he felt terrible about the way he had treated his wife. The Holy Spirit began to show him that Vi truly needed him. She was alone, trying to be mother, father, and counselor at the same time. She never would have called if it hadn't been a real emergency. She had sought his help and had had no idea he was in a meeting.

"I've got to call and apologize," he told himself. "I'll wait till tonight when the rates have gone down, and we can talk longer."

But all morning long, the Spirit kept prodding. By two o'clock on Saturday afternoon he could stand it no longer.

Erny phoned his wife and told her how sorry he was. They talked over their problems for a long time. He gave her the counsel and support and affirmation she needed.

That last thing he said was, "Vi, I want you to know that I love you. I really appreciate your letting me go to meetings like this."

At dusk that day, Vi took her bicycle out for a ride. She had gone less than half a mile when a drunken driver hit her from behind, throwing her 140 feet, breaking her neck and back. She died instantly.

That night Ed Kilbourne had to call his brother Erny with the news. He painfully told him what had happened.

"Ed, you must be wrong!" Erny said. "I just talked to Vi this afternoon!"

Afterward, Ed said to me, "Do you have any idea what that telephone call now means to Erny?"

17

The High Calling of Christian Parenthood

Now that we've skirted the pitfalls and scaled the high points of marriage—from the gleam-in-the-eye phase to the unconditional forgiveness phase—it is time to consider the ultimate purpose of all this. Parenthood.

In the Bible, parenthood is looked upon as a God-given privilege, a weighty responsibility, and a high and holy calling. It is an event which should bring great celebration and joy, as it did in the story of the birth of Samuel.

All of which contributes to the concept of the Covenant, the sacred agreement or commitment that God makes with man. In the Scriptures, He almost always makes that commitment with individuals, but solely in order to establish a *family covenant* and commitment.

It is a promise not to bless just an individual, but to bless his seed—his children and his children's children, even unto the third and fourth generations.

With our Western emphasis on individualism we tend to overlook this, but it is absolutely central to the main thrust of Scripture. This is why the Bible has those long lists of genealogies in the Old Testament, which so many of us find boring, because we don't realize how important they were to the men of those days. At that time almost all history was passed down by word of mouth from father to son and there was a tradition of tribal movement. A man's sense of permanence—of belonging to his place in time—depended in a large measure upon his knowledge of his family's lineage. That's why the word "family" or "families" appears more than a hundred times in the Book of Numbers, and the key phrase is, "So they set out every one by his family" (Numbers 2:34).

The longest family tree in the Bible, and perhaps anywhere, is the first nine chapters of I Chronicles. It starts with Adam and meticulously traces the line of descent all the way down to the time of the destruction of Judah. What it is trying to say is that, despite decay, downfall, division and destruction, they could still trace their ancestry back to the same family which in the time of Abraham had been united to God in a sacred covenant.

We don't have the same sense of urgency today about remembering who our ancestors were. But what we have to see is that the unity and integrity of our family is as important to God today as it was two, three, and four thousand years ago. It is perfectly in keeping with the spirit of the Scriptures when David Mace, the excellent writer on Christian marriage, says, "I solemnly believe that parenthood is the most God-like act of which man is capable."

When you look at parenthood in that light, you are forced to examine your motives for becoming a parent.

Even among Christians it is amazing how few really ask themselves the question: Why do we want to have children?

Is it just to keep up with the Jones's?

Is it because all the other couples in the neighborhood have children, so maybe we ought to have them too?

Do we regard children as extensions of our own personalities, or have them to project ourselves into another identity? If so, this may well produce a crippling kind of possessiveness, "smother" love, rather than mother love. And it often leads to the destruction of an individual, rather than to his fulfillment and completion.

Or have you had children just to satisfy the aching arms of motherhood or fatherhood and thus fill a deep psychological loneliness? If so, you will use your children merely as a means of loving yourself, and you will damage them badly in the process.

The Christian motivation for having children should go back to this high and holy calling to be a procreator, a creator on behalf of God, and can be stated something like this: just as God created His children as an expression of His love and for the extension of His own joy and blessedness, so a husband and wife should want to incarnate their love—and His—in their child. In this way, procreation takes on its fullest divine significance.

There's another reason why parenthood is such a high calling: Not only is it a call to create like God, *it is a call to love like God.* For God has delegated to man the power to love, as well as create.

Our first point makes it a *divine* call. The second makes it a *difficult* call, for we are to love our children the way God loves us.

Do we love our children unconditionally? Many parents may think so, but somehow their children get the feeling that their parents love them only when they are good and perfectly obedient.

Thus, as long as the children "behave," the parents love them very dearly. But let them be disobedient or displease their parents somehow, and see how they tend to reject them by withholding or withdrawing their love. Is this the way God loves us?

In Romans 5:6-10 God makes it clear that He cannot always approve of what we do. However, His love for us has never flagged for a moment. Indeed, God demonstrated the extent of His love for us at just such a time, when He sent His Son to die for us.

Can you and I love that way? It is not easy; naturally speaking, it's impossible. But we, as Christians, are called to love with His supernatural, "*agape* love"—the love which emanates directly from Him and never stops, no matter what.

Don't misunderstand me. I'm not advocating that we indulge our children or allow them to behave wrongly. That would hardly be love! God, for example, loves us so much that He is deeply concerned about the way we live. "For whom the Lord loves He reproves" (Proverbs 3:12).

Right here is perhaps the most difficult lesson we parents have to learn. How can we correct and discipline our children, even enforcing the discipline with punishment when necessary, without ever ceasing to love them and always making them feel we love them, regardless of what they may do?

Haim Ginott's bestseller, *Between Parent and Child,* makes an excellent point in regard to parents disciplining in love. They must make the distinction between correcting and disciplining a child for wrong behavior, and belittling him as a person. Be angry at his wrong conduct and correct him. But never cast aspersions on the child as a person.

It's the difference between saying, "*That thing* which you did was wrong, and I will not stand for that, because I love you too much to allow you to grow up with that kind of behavior," or saying to the child, "*You* are a naughty boy; *you* are a bad girl. *You* are a terrible person because you did such a thing."

You know what you've got here? A basic Biblical truth: hate the sin, but love the sinner.

How interesting that modern psychology has finally caught up with the Scriptures! We are called to discipline, but we must never despise, or even give a child the impression we do.

Hardly a week passes but that I spend time with someone who is desperately trying to believe God loves him, trying to accept His forgiveness, but he finds it almost an emotional impossibility because of experiences in his home. His parents loved him only when he was good and withdrew that love whenever he fell below a certain high standard.

I think perhaps the greatest legacy you can give your child is this experience of unconditional, God-like love. That kind of love is not possible on mere human terms; we don't get it from a book on parenthood or by setting our wills to love, or by recognizing our biological and sociological responsibilities. We get it by spending time on our knees with the Source of *agape* love.

How well I remember an incident when I was a small boy in India. My mother had crossed my will by not letting me do something I wanted to, and I sassed her. My dad's words at that moment are as clear today as they were then.

"David, march up those stairs."

Out of the corner of my eye, I could see dad taking off his belt as he followed me up the stairs. He then proceeded to correct my language by getting to the very seat of the trouble. But in the midst of my tears I was assured that he loved me and that he loved Mother, which was why he couldn't allow me to talk back to her.

This incident not only left an impression on a certain portion of my anatomy; it left a permanent impression on the anatomy of my spiritual life. Thus, I never had trouble understanding how God could love me, even when there were things in me of which He could not approve and for which He had to correct and chastise me.

What kind of a legacy are you giving your child? Is he forming a proper picture of his Heavenly Father through the lens of his earthly father and mother?

Finally, this high and holy calling of Christian parenthood is not only a call to create like God and to love like God, it is *a call to witness for God.*

Many kinds of evangelism are needed today. Mass evangelism is needed in certain quarters. Personal evangelism is always needed. Open air and street evangelism, I believe, are going to be more and more of a necessity, along with radio and television. We also need evangelism in literature, evangelism-in-depth, and a real intellectual evangelism to reach the minds of the world.

But perhaps the greatest need in the Christian church today is for a new emphasis on parental or family evangelism: the producing of strong Christian families. The only way this will be accomplished is through the witness of spiritually and emotionally mature parents.

We have talked about the church being the family of God. Now let's reverse it and remember that the *family* is the extension of the church of God. This is what the Book of Acts means when it talks about "the church in your house." The home is the extension of the church for day-by-day worship and the practice of Christian teachings.

The famous old camp meeting preacher, Uncle Bud Robinson, used to tell this story.

A woman was converted under his ministry. A few days later she came to Uncle Bud and said she felt God was calling her to preach. He asked her if she had any children.

"Oh, yes," she replied, "I have a large family!"

Uncle Bud's face lit up. "Well, bless God, Sister! He's not only called you to preach, He's given you a congregation as well!"

There is great theological truth in that. You parents have been called to witness, and you have been given a sanctuary and a congregation. For too long we have let the school and business and PTA and even our church activities come first. It's time that the family came first—even at the expense of the church.

Clearly, we must restore the Christian family to where the Bible puts it; in absolute first place among all human relationships.

When parents have carried their witness to children effectively—not by what they say to them or do to them, nearly so much as by the way they *are* with them— and children see the light and are in one spirit and accord with the parents in their devotion to living for Jesus, then you have an almost invincible witness in a community.

90

One of the most dramatic scenes in the Bible is the place where Joshua summoned all the heads of families and clans before him (Joshua 24).

He was getting on in years, and he wanted to know about the future course of Israel. He had reason to be concerned, for the Israelites had always had a weakness for worshiping other gods and betraying their covenant with the Lord.

As soon as they entered the Promised Land, they began to settle among the pagan Canaanites. Joshua knew too well the dangerous possibilities of infiltration, corruption, and growing compromise with idolatry.

So in that great moment at Shechem, Joshua stood before all the assembled heads of families and in ringing words reminded them of the mighty acts of God, who had always kept His promised covenant with them. He told them that a fateful choice faced them, and then he flung down his immortal challenge, "Choose for yourselves today whom you will serve" (Joshua 24:15).

Some of the older men wonder if Joshua, for all his authority, would be able to lead them much longer.

"Perhaps the wise thing is to worship with the Canaanites for the future security of the people," they said.

The younger ones, who had no memory of the great victories and shared hardships, frankly skeptical about the whole covenant business may have been saying, "Let's return to the old gods of Terah . . . . Ah, remember the gods of the Amorites, and the good harvests they gave . . ."

It seemed as though the steadfast families of the Lord were about to lose courage. It looked as if they were outnumbered. Suddenly above the clamor of their contention, Joshua raised his voice to a shout. In powerful, carrying tones he declared, "Choose for youselves today whom you will serve : . . . but as for me and my house, we will serve the Lord" (Joshua 24:15).

Electrifying. The people's cowardice and indecision

vanished. The issue was clear. There was only one way they could go. "And the people answered and said, 'Far be it from us that we should forsake the Lord to serve other gods' " (Joshua 24:16).

Can you imagine the shout that must have gone up?

A powerful leader, supported by his loyal family, had just made a tremendous impact for God. And the result? Amazing consequences which stood the test of time and are seen even in the second and third generation. Remember that in the early chapters of the next book it says, "And the people served the Lord all the days of Joshua" (Judges 2:7a). And better still, "And all the days of the elders who survived Joshua" (Judges 2:7b).

The longer I live, the more I believe in the idea of God's covenant relationship with families. The promise of Deuteronomy is that if we teach these things diligently to our children, then our days and the days of our children will have God's blessing upon them. This promise is also inferred in the Book of Acts: "Believe in the Lord Jesus, and you shall be saved, and your household" (Acts 16:31).

I believe when we are faithful to fulfill our high calling to Christian parenthood, then we have the scriptural authority to assume that God will be faithful in the fulfillment of His holy covenant with us. What a comfort this should be to the heart of every Christian parent!

18

Living It

It's time now to look at the way a functioning Christian family interacts.

There are three great fundamentals which every child gets from his or her parents and home.

First, the child gets his picture of himself; his self-image.

God had ordained this plan for the development of the person in a most remarkable way. Nine months before the child is born, he is carried inside his mother's body. He has no physical existence of his own. He feeds off her, breathes off her. Her bodily functions and organs have to function for both herself and the baby.

Slowly but surely, in what is the most breath-taking miracle of all, that baby develops a physical life of his own. Then comes the majestic act of creation that we call birth.

Life *begins* with this dramatic act of separation. The cord is severed and the child becomes a physically independent person. But he's still completely helpless and dependent, and as a person, he barely exists. He's a personality mostly in potential.

He becomes conscious of himself very gradually. At first he doesn't know the difference between himself and his blanket. He'll chew his big toe or the corner of the blanket, it doesn't matter which.

That child is going to discover his identity and who he is only in the mirror of the people around him. He has no existence, no identity other than what he sees reflected in their eyes, their voices and their attitudes. And what he sees mirrored there becomes his basic opinion of himself, the picture of himself that will profoundly affect the rest of his life.

At a recent small gathering a young minister was sharing his deep feelings of inadequacy and inferiority.

"I'm running scared all the time," he said. "I feel as though I can't do a thing successfully."

With honesty and openness, he went on to describe the bad picture he had of himself—a picture which happened to be totally different from ours.

Afterward a friend asked me, "What in the world would make such a brilliant, handsome, successful pastor feel that way about himself?"

I didn't reply. I happened to know the young man's parents and something of his upbringing. Often I had overheard the subtle belittling, the continual comparison with a beautiful successful older sister. I knew the source of this young man's deep sense of inferiority: his family.

Such tragedies are repeated over and over again. In the supermarket check-out lines, two mothers with two children stand waiting. One little child reaches to help mother put the things on the conveyor belt. Instinctively she responds.

"Watch out! You're going to break that! It's too heavy for you!"

The other mother responds differently.

"That's right. Put it there, honey. Thank you."

And she says proudly to the clerk, "He's my little helper. I really don't know what I'd do without him."

Right before our eyes we see two children developing two drastically different self-images. Parents, future parents! remember, you are the mirror in which your child will form his or her basic self-image, and no minister or counselor or psychiatrist can fully repair or replace what God intended the family to provide: love, security, and a sense of wholeness and belonging.

Second, a child receives in the family his attitude toward the basic realities of life.

The family is the testing laboratory where each child discovers the laws of life. A child is a natural tester; he experiments with different ways of behaving, of looking at life. He tries people. He tests parents. In the family laboratory, he will either learn that this is a moral, orderly universe and grow up with a healthy respect for law and order and reality, or else he will grow up in an unreal world, where he thinks you can have your cake and eat it, too.

That's why limitations are such a vital part of true love—why there has to be firmness and discipline at the heart of the family. Otherwise, the child grows up thinking he can make his own laws, set his own rules, play the game the way he wants to, when he wants to.

In contrast, the spoiled, unloved child creates his own kingdom, and makes himself king. Unfortunately the world takes a dim view of anyone who thinks he is the center of everything.

Earl Jabay works with disturbed patients in the New Jersey Neuro-psychiatric Institute, near Princeton. He has written two excellent books on this subject: *The Kingdom of Self* and *The God Players*. He makes the point that much emotional disturbance happens because people never learned limits. In plain English, that means they're willful, spoiled brats! They think they can play God; they don't acknowledge the limitations of the universe.

It is a tragic disservice to allow a child to develop this kind of unrealistic view of the world. It's like not teaching him about the law of gravity. One day he jumps out of a tall building and has a wonderful time—twentieth story, nineteenth, eighteenth—whee, it's fun to fly! Down,

down, down. The problem comes when he hits the sidewalk.

Limitations are vital realities every child needs to discover in the home, not later on some hard sidewalk of life.

Third (and most important of all) the child gets from his home his basic concept of God.

Home is like a window through which a child gets his first view of heavenly things. The ideas we get from our earthly mothers and fathers often determine how we regard our Heavenly Father.

A preacher's wife called me one day. Her husband had suffered a complete nervous breakdown, and she wanted me to talk to him. We met in a nearby city and went to the hospital where he was confined.

"I can't understand my husband," she said. "He seems to have a built-in slave driver, who drives and drives him. Everywhere we've gone, the congregations love Bill. But he doesn't think he's pleasing them. He can't believe they really love or appreciate him.

"So he works—and overworks. The church officials tell him, 'Brother Bill, you don't need to do all these things.' But he rushes around from this to that. He overloads himself, trying to please. Now he's had a breakdown."

I began to spend some time with the shattered minister. He started remembering and sharing some of the earliest experiences in his family. Like every normal boy, he wanted to please his mother and dad.

He tried to please his mother by helping around the house, setting the table. He'd get things ready, and she'd say, "No, the forks go over here." He'd fix them, then the knives would be wrong, then the salad plate, then the glasses. He could never do it right; Mother always had to come along behind and do it over.

Mothers and fathers ought to pray the missionary's prayer; "Lord, give me the grace to stand by and see a job sometimes poorly done." That's part of growth—the child's and the parents'. But Bill's mother was always on

96

him, till he finally gave up.

Bill's dad didn't have much education. He was reliving his own life through his son, so there was great emphasis on all areas of academic achievement. Bill was just an average student. Dad said, after one report card, "You know, I think if you were to work harder, really apply yourself, you could get all B's."

Bill wanted to please Dad, so he tried hard. There came a day when he ran home with his report card. There were B's on that card—there was even an A.

Dad looked at it and then said, "I think, Bill, with a little more effort, you could get all A's."

Bill was not that great a student, but he began knocking himself out and finally, after a long exhausting ordeal, his teachers congratulated him for a card that had nothing but A's on it. He ran home to show Dad.

Dad opened it, looked, and then said casually, "Yes, but these teachers always give A's, don't they?"

When Bill grew up he exchanged one mother and dad for five hundred people in his congregation. From his point of view, he simply could not please them, though his wife had assured me otherwise.

He told me, "It's like God is on the top of the ladder and I'm trying to climb up to Him to please Him, but I never can! I try as hard as possible but He's up there, and He's asking for more. So I climb up one rung then another and another. My knuckles are bleeding and my shins are bruised. Finally I'm about to reach Him and now I'm *really* going to please Him. But then He moves up another three rungs."

Some of us wonder why we live under a cloud of guilt and anxiety. Maybe it doesn't have a thing to do with God or conscience. Maybe the fault is back there—where we grew up.

I am thankful I had the kind of father who made it the easiest, most natural thing in the world for me to believe in a loving Heavenly Father.

19

Christ Is the Head

What kind of family structure do we need?

The first Scripture we ought to look at is Ephesians 5:21: "Be subject to one another in the fear of Christ." Don't, I repeat, *don't* start the passage on the family with "Wives, be subject to your own husbands (Ephesians 5:22), because the true head of the home is the God who is revealed to us in Jesus Christ. God has a pattern for the family structure. It does not begin with the husband or wife, but with Himself; with mutual surrender and submission to a Higher Authority than either one.

Many men make a one-sided and extreme application of this Scripture. There has been a resurgence of this idea recently. Any man who is trying to force his wife to submit to him has never started at the beginning. *Both partners submit to each other because they have already submitted to Jesus Christ.*

What's next in the pattern?

The role of husband and wife. "Wives, be subject to your own husbands, as to the Lord" (Ephesians 5:22). The husband is the head of the wife as Christ is the Head of the Church.

This introduces a whole, new element: Christ, the Lord of the Church, did not "lord it over" the Church! He got down on His hands and knees and washed His disciples' feet! He emptied Himself and made Himself of no reputation. He told us in Luke 22:25-27 that we are not to exercise lordship as do the pagans.

Some men, when they use the word "head," think of head-man, like the victor in a power struggle, or a Mr. Big who boasts of being the head of the company, with authority over thirty men.

That is not what is meant in Ephesians! The role of the husband is something very different: *Husbands, love your wives, just as Christ also loved the Church and gave Himself up for her* (Ephesians 5:25). "Nevertheless let each individual among you also love his own wife even as himself; and let the wife see to it that she respect her husband" (Ephesians 5:33).

Behind the analogy of Christ and His Church is something even more basic: the Trinity, the very structure of the character of God.

God is One in Three Persons. In the Trinity, the Son is equal to the Father, but subservient to the Father. Now *there* is the key to the whole Biblical family pattern. Christ the Son, the second Person in the Trinity, is equal to the Father, but subservient to His authority. There's no question of superiority or inferiority here. In Christ, male and female, husband and wife, are equal. And under Christ, *both submit to one another, because they have first submitted to Him.*

When it comes down to the daily life of the family, the Biblical pattern is clear. The husband is the final authority, and the wife is to submit to him.

I don't like to use the word "law," but I'm going to do it deliberately. When the wife is under the law of the husband, the husband is under the law of love: self-sacrificing love, which Christ exemplified on the cross. Who do you think is under the more severe law, husband or wife?

If husbands would stick to that kind of authority, the vast majority of wives would respond in respect and submission. The fact of the matter is, the husband's authority is also spelled as responsibility: self-giving, sacrificial love, responsible for wife and family.

Studies show that deep down in every woman's heart she's looking for this kind of a head to respond to. The tragedy is, so many women say, "Pastor, how do you submit to a bowl of jello? How can I be subservient to a jellyfish?"

Centuries ago, Chrysostom, the great silver-tongued orator of the ancient church, preached a sermon on this text. He asked, "But what if my wife reverence me not? Never mind, *thou* art to love. Fulfill thy own duty."

I believe that with all my heart. Some books and teachings on the Christian home infer from the Ephesians passage that the Christian husband has a right to say, "Look here! The Bible says you're to submit to me, and you're going to submit to me, whether you like it or not!"

Can you imagine Jesus yelling those words at His disciples, who were in the early Church?

There's nothing in Ephesians, or anywhere else in Scripture for that matter, about forcing your wife to submit. It is the wife's responsibility to submit to the respect and authority of her husband. If she does not, that is a matter for her to settle with God. And you, Mr. Husband, have not been relieved of your responsibility to love her with Christlike, self-giving love—regardless of what she does.

To be a really strong Christian family, strong in the Lord, we must have God's pattern of authority in operation.

Today we've gone from one extreme where fathers used to be monarchs and tyrants to the other extreme, where now we have wholesale abdication from leadership in the home on the part of husbands and fathers. We are reaping the harvest of this massive, male cop-out. Family anarchy has resulted. The father has become Mr. Nobody.

He's the seconder of the motion, "You heard what your mother said."

Or he's the sergeant-at-arms, "Do what your mother tells you!"

Or, the greatest cop-out of all, "Ask your mother."

My greatest plea in the day-to-day realities of family relationships is, *Husbands, take your rightful role in the family. Be father in fact.* Whatever the sacrifice this requires in time, in business, in success, make it! *You must obey God's directives.*

God's pattern of authority is all one piece. First Christ. Then husband and wife in mutual submission to Him and to each other. The husband: protective, responsible, authoritative. The wife: loving, responsive, respectful. You can't break the chain at one link and then expect it to work at the next.

The next verse says, "Children, obey your parents in the Lord, for this is right" (Ephesians 6:1). Now the husband and wife are a team. In relation to their children they are one, no longer two. To obey them—the team— is the duty of the child. In unity, husband and wife share authority over the children.

Do you see why it's so important, Dad and Mother, that you get together on discipline, and not let the children divide you?

The Biblical pattern calls for the enforcing of discipline. No equality! There is parental authority and children's obedience. "Honor your father and your mother" (Exodus 20:12) is the foundation of the Christian home. It's not only the first Commandment with promise, it's the first Commandment with consequences attached to it.

As we saw in the first chapter, there is no greater test of your Christian life and parenthood than the way you handle this matter of discipline. It reveals what you think about God, your children, your family, and yourself.

My philosophy of child-rearing in a nutshell is this: start discipline early, the earlier the better. If you young parents think you're going to let your child be completely on his own when he's small and then expect to teach him when he becomes a teen-ager, you are in for one of the rudest shocks of your life.

I visit in homes and watch the little tyrants. (When you don't follow God's hierarchy, you get anarchy—child rule. That's what we have in much of America today.) I watch that "cute" little boy. He's literally tearing up the place. I'm trying to have a pastoral visit, and he's defying the household like a little Napoleon.

That adorable little girl, she's so pretty and dressed so beautifully. She's having a tantrum, emotionally blackmailing the whole household to yield to her whims. Mother and Dad smile and say to the Pastor, "Aren't they cute kids?"

You may consider that cute when they're small. But that little tyrant of two, three or four will be the rebellious, disobedient teen-ager who will someday break your heart.

Start early. That's the secret. Be strict with your small child. Give him lots of love and plenty of affection, but also set plain limits, enforcing them in whatever way is necessary.

You will be astounded at how quickly you can then give him freedom. As he grows up, you can turn him loose surprisingly soon—if you've been an enforcer of limits at an early age. Then you'll be happy to see how responsible a decision he'll be able to make on his own.

I'll never forget a crisis day in my son's life. He was about five years old when he decided he was going to take over the home. I took off my belt and took him upstairs and got to the seat of the problem. He went right back and started again. So I took him back upstairs again. Five times I had to do this!

A relative of ours was there that day. She said, "David, I have never seen anything so cruel in my life."

I said, "Keep out of this, please. It's between father and son."

Don't think this was easy. It tore my heart. I was

churning inside. But every time I told him in real love, "Steve, you cannot do this. I love you too much to allow you to do this. I run the family, and you don't."

That was a turning point in his attitudes. Years later, when Steve was a man, he heard me tell this story. "Dad," he said, "I don't even remember that time."

There are three ingredients of love for the daily realities of disciplining and loving.

First, *understanding*.

Read a good book specifically on child care, so that you know what to expect of your child at every level of his life. This is important, because if you over-expect you will probably over-correct. Paul admonishes us not to over-correct, or we'll goad our children into resentment.

Second, *availability*.

There's only one gift one human being can give to another: time. Those of us in Christ's service are often the worst offenders here. We save the world, give time to others, but not to our own family.

During the growing years of our children when I felt my relationship with them was shaky, I sometimes put a sign on my office door.

"An emergency has arisen. The Pastor is unavailable. Watch for future announcement."

I have taken from one to three days and not gone back until I saw that things had been restored to the correct pattern at home. Be available when they want you, need you. "Later on" is too late.

Third, *a sensitive, listening ear*.

How important! Kids are like snowflakes—no two of them alike. You discover their differences by listening. I don't know why teen-agers invariably want to talk to you when you're dead tired, crawling into bed.

A sheepish look, "Daddy, can I talk to you?"

"Sure, honey, I'll just be a minute."

But it pays. This letter that a son wrote to his father is evidence.

"Dear Dad,

"Well, Father's Day has come and gone, and as I usually do, I forgot to call or send you a card. But as I sit here in the office, I can't help but think about all the things you and Mom have done for me. I guess I never really appreciated you all the way I should have when I was at home. But having lived here for a while now, and seeing all the paganism, both inside the church and out, I realize how lucky I was to have you for parents.

"In working with some of the young people, it's more like paddling a boat upstream, because I get no support whatever from their homes. I have to admire some of these kids. They have all the initiative themselves. When I look back on it, I don't think I ever had a chance to go wrong. Sure, we had our ups and downs, but I always knew you loved me, and I never lost respect for you. How fortunate I am!

"As I think about your life, I see a lot of parallels with mine. I look at these years here, both as years of ministry, but also as years of preparation, for a task God has for me, ahead. I know I have a long way to go. God is going to have to break me a lot more before He can use me the way He wants to, but thank you for helping me this far. I just hope I can be half the father to Matthew that you were and still are to me."

It's signed "Steve"—my own son. And I wouldn't take a million dollars for that letter.

SHARE THE WEALTH
WITH YOUR FRIENDS
WITH LOW COST
NEW LEAF LIBRARY BOOKS

The Wonderful Way of Living

Christian Life

One of the most talked about inspirational magazines today . . . Colorful personality profiles . . . skilled analyses of world trends in light of the Bible . . . Poignant narratives . . . wide ranging reports on the latest in helpful books and records.

Membership in Christian Life brings you this exciting monthly magazine plus Ten Additional Bonus Features including discounts on the best in books and records.

ORDER NOW AND SAVE

☐ Yes, please enter a membership in Christian Life for twelve months for $9 (for foreign subscriptions add $3 per year for postage).

Name_____

Address_____

City_____State_____Zip____

☐ Enter or extend a two year membership at $16 (you save $2).

☐ Enter or extend a membership for three years at $21 (you save $6).